A GROUP PHOTOGRAPH

BEFORE, NOW & IN-BETWEEN

—

Andrew Tatham

Arvo Veritas

CREDITS

Publication

Text   Andrew Tatham
Foreword   Piet Chielens

Publisher   Arvo Veritas (www.arvoveritas.co.uk) - 1st Edition published by In Flanders Fields Museum

Layout   Manu Veracx for B.AD

Translation   Marc Hutsebaut for Tinseltown v.o.f.

Photo credits

The artefacts were photographed by Jan D'Hondt for B.AD. The majority of the photographs came from the families who kindly provided them or allowed me to copy them for the purposes of this project. Other photographs taken by Andrew Tatham, Johann Asirvadem, Gilles Medalin-Moret, Rachel Pearce. It has been very difficult to contact all copyright holders – please contact andrew@groupphoto.co.uk with any copyright queries related to material in this book.

Tea in the Garden, National Trust Images (p.83)
The revolver in William Walton's stained glass window, Rama, Wikimedia Commons, Cc-by-sa-2.0-fr (p.176)
Pugh appears courtesy of The Daily Mail (p.200)

Legal Deposit (Royal Library of Belgium): D/2015/6486/2
ISBN: 978-0-9935302-0-3 (1st Edition: 978-9-0902927-8-6)

Exhibition

A Group Photograph. Before, Now & In-between.
A History & Art Project by Andrew Tatham.
In Flanders Fields Museum (27/09/2015 – 3/01/2016)

Layout   Manu Veracx for B.AD

Production   Movies produced by Klaus Verscheure for Danse la Pluie

For the In Flanders Fields Museum: Piet Chielens, Ivan Claerebout, Els Deroo, Birger Stichelbaut, Annick Vandenbilcke, Frederik Vandewiere, Margot Brulard, Lidia Giacomini and Margaret Harris

Lenders   This exhibition would never have been realized without the trust of the families who loaned us their memorabilia.
The Wardrobe, Regimental Museum of the Royal Berkshire Regiment, in Salisbury (UK).

IN FLANDERS FIELDS MUSEUM

Cloth Hall - Grote Markt 34 - B 8900 Ypres - Belgium - www.inflandersfields.be

A GROUP PHOTOGRAPH

BEFORE, NOW & IN-BETWEEN

Andrew Tatham

A Picture of Men in a War

I was in a pub
There was a picture of men in a war
I thought about the picture
I did nothing

I went to the museum
There were moving pictures of men in a war
I read about war
I looked at my family

I saw my great-grandfather
In a picture of men in a war
I read about the tears in his eyes
I felt tears in my eyes

And now I search
That picture of men in a war
I see today and yesterday
I cannot forget

Royal Berkshire dragon carved in chalk from the 1st Line of German Trenches
captured by the 8th Royal Berkshires at the Battle of Loos.

CONTENTS

FOREWORD

If you have ever shown any interest in the First World War, you are bound to have come across pictures of groups of men or – sometimes, though much less often – women. Groups of people in uniform, looking decently, solemnly, serenely, seriously into the lens so as not to disturb the decent, solemn, serene, in short, important occasion for which the photograph was being made. As individuals, they are utterly secondary to the group they belong to. Negligible, replaceable. And never more so than in times of war. Whenever there's a loss, the group is patched up until it's good to go again, ready to continue playing its role in the war. Or as Jean Giono would have it: *"[My] company was a small measure of capacity of the division, like a bushel of grain. When the bushel of men was empty or only a few were left, like grains sticking to the seams, it was replenished with new men. Thus, the company was filled a hundred times and a hundred times more. And a hundred times it was emptied underneath the millstone again."*

Battles in any war are still being described as if the units partaking in them are the actual personae, rather than the individuals who make up the motley groups; like football teams whose glory is as imperishable as the pitch they are entering. Players can be replaced, but the team lives on. And we, the audience that is interested in the history of these groups of people, are scarcely better behaved than supporters. Our Score! Our Colours! *Our Boys,* Them or Us, *Gott mit Uns, With God on Our Side! Die Hards* they are called, or *Diables Bleus, Green Berets* or *Blue Helmets*.

In his impressive study of one single group photograph which shows the officers whom his great grandfather had trained for the First World War, Andrew Tatham has left the team behind and reduced the group to the level of the individual once more. He hasn't just researched the lives of each of the 46 men from the 8th Battalion of the Royal Berkshire Regiment. Using each man's date of birth as a starting point, he has gone back and forward one hundred years to look for their ancestors and their descendants, to trace their timelines within the great, violent times which have marked their and our past and present.

Over twenty years of research yielded so many different types of data that Andrew had to devise new ways of processing and communicating them. In his mind his historical research quickly took on the form of an art project. But finding the right expression for each of his datasets proved a long-winded process, spanning many years. He made an animated movie which plotted the concept of growing family trees on a timeline. Years later, those highly schematic trees received a makeover, with the lives of ancestors and descendants now elegantly dancing on the tide like branches of a lush mangrove forest. Andrew also collected as many portrait pictures of each of the men as he could. Collating these pictures in a montage resulted in

yet another imagining of "time". But it often didn't prove sufficient to represent "their time". As it is, there are usually no pictures of those lifetime events that are the most dramatic, often darkest ones. So Andrew started creating designs for stained glass portraits recalling precisely those events in each man's life. Obviously, the stained glass window isn't such an omnipresent shape in the commemoration by accident.

What's the purpose of this all? And why should a museum about the First World War use this material to organize an exhibition? Andrew Tatham's study pertains to an almost utterly random group of people. Take the example of South African brothers Charlie and Leslie Berlein. Many of their personal items have been preserved without knowing which object belonged to whom exactly. They are all shown together a bit further on in this book, which only tells the story of Leslie, because he happened to be in the group photograph. Which could just as well have been a group photograph with the slightly older Charlie Berlein. Instead of the 8th Royal Berkshires going to Loos, the book would then have been about the 5th Ox & Bucks going to Ypres, with Charlie Berlein falling as the first of his unit and the first of 473 men from that unit who would perish at Ypres. The dates, the numbers, the places don't matter at all. Andrew's elaborate study of this particular group photograph is just as relevant and direct in showing the devastating and lasting impact of the war on any other group. More than half these men died in the war, many others were wounded and even during the later, often rich lives led by the survivors and their descendants, the war continues to resonate. Andrew Tatham reminds us of that at least four times, times 46.

In the face of wartime destruction and death he erects a celebration of life, in all its abundance and elusiveness, as well as simplicity. Andrew's endlessly repetitive mangroves are like the trees of life from Jean Giono's *L'homme qui plantait des arbres*: the man who plants trees, every single one of which is a life and gives life and keeps on giving.

Andrew Tatham and I share a mutual admiration for the great French novelist and war veteran. In 1934 Giono wrote: *"They will never be able to console us for the war… Which is why I have so impetuously chosen the side of the trees, the animals and the snow."*

Andrew Tatham is on the side of the trees and, in doing so, provides us with insight and solace. For that, he deserves our great thanks and appreciation.

Piet Chielens,
In Flanders Fields Museum, Ieper

INTRODUCTION

What do you see when you look at this group photograph? Do you see soldiers ready to fight or victims of war? Or do you see sons and brothers and husbands and fathers and grandsons and nephews and friends? Do you see the artist, the champagne merchant, the medical student or the music critic? When I first saw this picture, I saw my great-grandfather in the centre. He was the commanding officer of the 8th Battalion Royal Berkshire Regiment and having read his letter from the battlefield of Loos, I had an idea of the horrors that befell the men in this picture. And looking around those faces all sorts of questions came to mind:

What happened to them all?
Did they know what they were getting into?
Where had they all come from?
Who was thinking about them as they sat there?
Who was worrying about them?
Who loved them?
What was the effect of the War on them and their families?
How are they remembered?

This exhibition is my way of trying to answer these questions. I've spent 21 years researching in archives and online, finding these men's relatives and visiting them in 23 counties in England as well as Scotland, Ireland, South Africa, Canada, America, & Australia and corresponding with people in Hong Kong, New Zealand, Argentina, Switzerland, all around the world and all the while hoovering up information and photographs and artefacts. It has been very difficult to do but what has driven me is wanting to make the artworks that are in this exhibition.

When I started out contacting the families I didn't know what I would find. And what I found was the most amazing window on the world – all sorts of little time capsules into other places and other times and other lives. There was a lot of pain and death, but there were also sparks of life and it was always a joy to find more pictures of these men particularly if they showed them as children or smiling or as old men with their grandchildren - and there are so many objects with stories behind them, stories of loss and love and survival. A lot of my aim has been to go from that original picture of soldiers and show the fullness of them as human beings, and to place them within the wider view of the World and Time. Some of this is possible through the traditional methods of telling stories and showing pictures and artefacts, but I have also developed ways of displaying the information and material I have collected so that new angles can be seen and new connections made. Not all of these can be shown in this book - exhibitions allow a scale and possibilities that cannot fit on paper - but I will describe everything and hope there will be other opportunities for you to experience them.

Animated film
The group photograph is one moment in time and as a way of showing the place of that moment in history I have made an animated film which shows all of the men's family trees growing over 136 years, mixed in with photos of their families and historical time markers and contemporary music for each year, as well as with the cycles of the moon and the seasons. Each of their trees grows like a real tree, with a trunk for each man and branches appearing for children, grandchildren and so on down the generations. There is a baby's cry for each birth, and a bell toll for each death. You can vividly see the immediate effect of the War on this group of men and get a view on the aftermath. This film forms the heart of the presentations I have been giving about my project for the last 10

years - and it is the enthusiastic response to these presentations that has been vital in encouraging me to continue my work.

Tree Drawings

A few years ago records started coming online that allowed me to extend the idea of the animated film and to not just show their descendants but also their ancestors going back 100 years before the First World War. I also thought it was important to give an idea of what happened to the families of those who were killed without having children, so I included the descendants of their brothers and sisters as well. I like to imagine their parents sitting at the table and asking their children "what do you want to be when you grow up?" and this is a way of showing that. Some trees died out a long time ago, whilst others have proliferated hugely. In amongst this positive picture of regeneration it's important to remember that all these new lives are holders for the past — even though the pain and loss were not talked about, it affected how people behaved, and that behaviour is passed down through the generations, often in ways we do not understand.

In order to be able to connect into the drawings and see that each root and branch is a thinking, breathing, feeling life, I have written annotations which tell you people's names and something of what they have done with their lives (or what life has done to them). To allow these to be to be easily readable, and also to give the whole installation an impact and a largeness of life, these tree drawings are printed 1 metre high and extend for over 34 metres along the walls of a corridor through the exhibition. That just cannot be translated into a book of this size (which is frustrating, given the fundamental importance of this work to my project), but the accompanying poster at least gives you an idea of the range of unique shapes of the trees - and you can view the trees online (and zoom in on the branches to see the details) via www.groupphoto.co.uk/extra (which also includes the example tree which explains how the trees work).

It is a large and complex picture, but at its core are some simple truths. We all have been made by countless people who for the most part we know little about and in turn we have the potential to create new lives that we cannot imagine - and we are all of one Earth and above us is one Sun. In the busyness and material pressures and pleasures of daily life it is easy to forget the fundamental truths of our existence that we all share. Drawing these trees has been like a form of meditation which helps to ground me and remind me of the miracle of birth and the strangeness of death, though I am no nearer to understanding either.

Photomontages

What you will see here is every single picture I have found of these men — in some cases it is just a handful because their family didn't really take pictures, or there isn't any family left or albums have been lost or destroyed. But in many cases I have been surprised by the number of pictures particularly of some of those who were killed in the war. Look at these pictures and you see so much about the history of photography over the last 150 years. In the begin everything is formality but as handheld cameras come in with shorter exposure times possible and lower costs, you start to see the beginnings of informal photography which allows more candid moments and fleeting expressions to be captured, enabling us to see more of the personalities behind the faces. It's interesting how valuable these pictures feel in comparison with the huge volume of photos being taken now in the digital age. Each photomontage is a memento of their whole life on Earth and also includes their signatures, medals, graves, and memorials where I've been able to find them. Some of the memorials deserve more space and have their own special section in this book.

Stained Glass Portraits

Most of the pictures I have found of these men are in black and white and show a very limited view of their lives. I wanted to add colour and depth and to make something that spoke of their uniqueness as a human being and of their spirit. It also struck me that the horrors they endured are almost undocumented and I felt it was important to in some way show the reality of their experience of War, in many cases the defining experience of their lives. Each of these portraits is a combination of many things, showing the inconstancy and variety of life and its emotions. There are elements of a code behind the colours and shapes and other characteristics of the pictures but I've also just done things because they felt right. Most of what we are as humans is hidden from other people and I wanted to keep a sense of that mystery. These are my subjective impressions and have been made with each man in turn being at the centre of my attention. In the exhibition they form part of a monumental installation, lit from behind and surrounded by the sounds accompanying the breaking of dawn in one of the cemeteries on the anniversary of the Battle of Loos.

A New Group Photograph

It has long been my dream to take a new group photograph to show the relatives of these men living today, and as I write this preparations are in place to bring together over 150 representatives of the families of 22 of the men, including over 20% of the living descendants of these men. People are coming from as far afield as Canada and South Africa to attend the Centenary commemorations for the Battle of Loos and be part of this new group photograph. It says something that they made the effort to travel all the way to Ypres at an awkward time of year. I'm really looking forward to seeing the resulting picture as I know that there are some very strong family likenesses in families and I wonder if people comparing this with the original Group Photograph will be able to work out who is related to whom. We are also using time-lapse photography to show everyone gathering for the photograph, having the new group photograph taken, and then leaving to go back to their normal lives outside of this - modern technology allows us to make it into a fuller artwork and put a contemporary twist on the original. Sadly this gathering of the families is happening the day before the opening of the exhibition so the new Group Photograph cannot appear in this book, but again it will be available online.

This Book

It has been absolute torture putting this book together because it has mostly consisted of discarding huge amounts of interesting material that I have collected, and I feel a responsibility to the memory of these men and to their relatives. In the end there just is not the time or the space to include everything, and I have aimed to focus on what is unique to this project. There are many military history books that tell the story of the War and when choosing items for this book my main criterion has been to show the effect of the War on these men and their families.

There are so many more stories still to tell, not least about the experience of doing this project, but that will have to wait for another book. In the meantime, I hope that what you see opens a window on the world that you have not seen before.

THEIR SHARED HISTORY

The Group Photograph presents a uniform body of men and that might give the idea that they had similar backgrounds and life experiences, and that they knew each other well. In fact the shared history of this group is remarkably limited and brief. Some of these men had joined the Battalion only weeks before the photograph was taken in May 1915, and even before they went to France at the beginning of August, some had left for other units and one, Harold Cohen, had died as a result of illness brought on by the strenuous training.

Background & Before
In looking at how they came to be in the picture, let's start with their backgrounds. You can explore their individual details on the roots and branches of the tree drawings, but here is a brief overview.

Geography & Race: Although on their application forms they had to confirm that they were "British born or a naturalised British subject" and "of pure European descent", and the majority were born in England (with many from the South East), there were some whose first experience of the world was in Scotland, Argentina, Ireland, India, Burma, Canada, and South Africa. Some of their parents were of German, Greek, Italian, Uruguayan, American, and Polish origin. Only 6 of them were born in the Berkshire that gave the Regiment its name.

Class: How does one define class? It is difficult to be precise but it has something to do with your family's background, with how your father earns (or doesn't earn) his living, with how much money you have, and with the circles in which your family moves. Traditionally there was an officer class from which the vast majority of Army officers came, with only a few having worked their way up from the ranks. But for the War and the need for massive expansion of the Army, a lot of these men would not have been able to become officers. In fact this was denoted by their commission being termed a "temporary commission" and this led to Regular Army officers referring to them as "temporary gentlemen". Probably no more than a third of these men would have been considered for commissions in the peace-time Army. Looking further back in their history and two thirds of their grandfathers would not have been considered to be of officer class. It just shows that there were possibilities of advancement in the Victorian era, though old money and breeding still counted to a great degree. You can get an idea of their range of backgrounds from the occupations of their fathers, who included an explorer, a tobacconists' traveller, the first Bishop in Persia, a biscuit factory machinist, an egg merchant, a gardener's labourer, and a physics professor.

Education: The archetype of the British Army officer is that he was a product of public school, and whilst there are representatives of Eton, Harrow, Rugby, Radley, Merchant Taylor's, Tonbridge, and Charterhouse here, there are also grammar school boys and some who attended smaller local schools near to their homes. I also know of three who spent the last year or two of their schooling in Germany, being sent on the train aged 16 and having no-one speak English to them after the first 3 weeks - a great recipe for fluency - and there were at least half a dozen fluent German and/or French speakers in this group. After school, several went on to University (including Oxford, Cambridge, London, Leeds, and University College Reading) whilst others attended agricultural colleges (at Wye, and Hawkesbury, New South Wales) or technical institutes (at Camborne School of Mines, and the Central Technical Institute South Kensington). Just under half of them went straight from school into the world of work.

Friendships: Some of them had connections before the War. Louis Klemantaski & Tod Hobbs were at University College School together, David Glen & Hugh Cassels were on the same Engineering course in London, and then there is a group of the senior officers who were all members of the Badminton Club in Piccadilly: Douglas Hanna, Douglas Tosetti, Ronald Brakspear and Charles Bartlett (these last three definitely being friends, with drink being a connection - respectively they were a champagne merchant, a brewery director and "a damn fine host").

Ages: Looking around the faces, you might get an idea of maturity (partly the uniform, partly the serious expressions, partly the moustaches), but actually just over half of them are aged 23 or under, with the youngest being 18 and the oldest, my great-grandfather, being 50.

Occupations before the War: When war broke out, two were still at school, with others also studying at University, whilst, in addition to the several businessmen (working in trades from advertising to brewing to tobacco to silk importing), there were teachers, lawyers, a vicar, an artist, a music critic, and a clerk working at Huntley and Palmers biscuit factory. Several travelled from around the globe to join up – a rancher in South Africa, a rubber planter in Malaya, a tea planter in Ceylon, an accountant in Canada, and a worker in a saw mill in the wilds of Canada.

Military Experience: Many of them had had some form of military training, whether it be in the Officers Training Corps at School or University or in their local Territorial Force unit. Three had served during the Boer War: Wilfred Oldman (with the Ceylon Mounted Infantry and then finishing as a sergeant in the South African Constabulary); James Barrow (with the Army Pay Corps as part of a full career from which he had retired as a warrant officer - and now on re-enlisting found himself a commissioned officer and quartermaster); and Ronald Brakspear (as a Captain in the Royal Bucks Militia who spent the two years of the Boer War in Ireland). Only two had seen regular service as officers. Charles Bartlett had bought himself out as a Lieutenant in 1906 after six years with the Royal Berkshires (serving in Gibraltar, Dublin, Egypt & Woking (!)). The other was my great-grandfather, Colonel William Walton. He had had a full 30 year career in the Indian Army, and although he was a renowned trainer of men, the only operational soldiering he had seen was during the Third Burma War of 1885-87 (right at the start of his service), and in the Persian Gulf in 1911.

Formation & Training

At the time war was declared, my great-grandfather William Walton was at home unemployed having handed over command of his battalion out in India in February 1914. He was a Colonel aged 50 and probably heading for retirement. The story my Gran told to me was that, sick of being given nothing to do, he got in touch with Lord Kitchener, who he knew from his time in India, and said, "Get me to do something, even if it's to serve as a private." And here in his own words is what happened next:

The 8th Battalion were raised at the Barracks, Reading, towards the end of September 1914. Colonel W C Walton, Indian Army, took over command at Codford training camp in the first week of October 1914. The Battalion was detailed as Army Troops and attached to the 26th Division. It was some time before any uniforms were received, and, owing to the absence of tent boards, the discomfort due to the plentiful rain was considerable. These and many other difficulties were happily overcome and training of officers & men proceeded. Besides the Commanding Officer there was only one other officer Major (then Captain) Bartlett who had any previous Regular Service. The latter was appointed Adjutant.

Some of the young officers had been in Officers' Training Corps. All worked with utmost zeal & keenness to learn and to impart instruction.

In November the Battalion was moved into billets in Reading, where steady progress was made in training with dummy rifles in the field, and with miniature rifles on the range. Owing to the patriotism & kindness of owners & farmers the Battalion was able to practise field manoeuvres in every direction in the vicinity of the town, and the municipality placed the swimming baths at the disposal of the Battalion on certain days of the week. The Battalion attended Divine Service every Sunday at St Giles', Reading, and afterwards used to march to billets by way of the Park, practising Battalion drill there on the way. Whilst at Reading the messing system was perfected. Major Bartlett was appointed 2nd-in-command & Lt TG Peacock Adjutant. The Battalion deservedly earned a good reputation in the town, where it remained until May 1915.

Early in May the Battalion moved to camp in hutments at Sutton Veney near Warminster, where Brigade & Divisional training was carried out with the 26th Division. At the end of July 1915 orders were received to embark for France on 7th August. New uniforms, rifles, machine guns and field equipment were issued, and the battalion was put through range practices for the first time with rifles, during the last ten or twelve days.

This gives quite a gentle view of things that belies his belief in strict discipline and strenuous and rigorous training (as you can imagine from the picture on the left). A good idea of what it was like to be on the receiving end of this, and of the realities of what it was like in those days can be seen in this account written many years later by Cecil Cloake:

The first picture of the 8th Royal Berkshires, in Boyton Park Camp, with William Walton in the centre - to his right are Charles Bartlett & James Barrow (in whose memorabilia this was found).

I joined the Battalion at Boyton Camp, Codford – oh! what a dismal experience. The whole unit, as it existed, was in very poor shape. Living in tents in more or less continuous rain and thick mud, some of the men wearing their civilian clothes and some others in the thin shoddy dark blue uniforms which had been issued to them. They were wet, cold and miserable and had no facilities for drying either themselves or their clothing. The officers too slept two in a tent and the mess was a leaky marquee, where we fed off an enamel plate and drank out of an enamel mug, without saucer.

I was posted to "C" Company and put in command of No 10 Platoon. Morale was so low that a few days later the men refused to go on parade. Little did they realise that this was open mutiny in time of war! However, Major Charles F N Bartlett – the 2nd in Command of the Battalion mounted his beautiful charger, "Punch" and arraigned the assembled men; promising that in a short time they would be moved, by train, to billets in Reading. This pleased the men very much as most of them came from that district.

The men, of course, at this time had no equipment, and drilled with broomsticks as rifles.

In about a week we struck camp and entrained for Reading, much to everyone's relief. Here the men were accommodated in various large halls and the officers took over the hotel portion of a large general stores in the main road – McIlroy's Hotel. Here we slept in beds, two in a room, and the large restaurant was taken over as the mess for all officers. From this crude and unpromising beginning gradually the Battalion was built up; frequent new drafts of men arrived and often one saw a new face in the Officers' Mess. Gradually too, uniforms and equipment arrived – but not rifles.

Training was the order of the day, and it was intensive and strenuous. Colonel W C Walton did not lay great stress on ordinary drill, but his strong point was field work and manoeuvre – "open warfare".

Daily we marched out by companies to Caversham Park to carry out bayonet fighting with broom sticks, physical training, platoon and company extended order drill, scouting and skirmishing. Midday meal of bread and cheese was carried and we stayed out until tea time, in all weathers.

Then after a whole day spent out of doors; sometimes in rain, cold wind or even snow, returning tired, hungry and exhausted, the officers were

treated, after the evening meal, to a lecture by the C.O. for an hour, in the mess, from "Infantry Training".

Looking back on those days I am sure that he was determined to make his 8th Royal Berkshires the most efficient battalion in the New Army, and, in my opinion, by the time we arrived in France he had succeeded.

Taking the Group Photograph

Sandhill Camp (also known as No. 12 in the Sutton Veny group of camps) was in Longbridge Deverill, near Warminster, Wiltshire. It was here that the Group Photograph was taken in May 1915, soon after the 8th Royal Berkshires moved down from Reading. All I know about the photographer is that he worked for the well-known portrait studio *Elliott & Fry*. Their records were destroyed during the Blitz in the Second World War and there the trail goes cold. The person whose work led to the remembrance of the men in the Group Photograph has ironically been forgotten by history himself.

The photograph below is a view of Sandhill Camp taken from Cow Down. Cow Down is the flat expanse of hillside you can see behind the men in the Group Photograph - as in the above "hats on" version that was taken at the same sitting as the one I've been working from. The camp was built from scratch in 1915, dismantled after the War, rebuilt for the Second World War, and now is back to fields again.

The marker "I sleep here" was written on this postcard and sent by Gordon Peacock to his sister Coline.

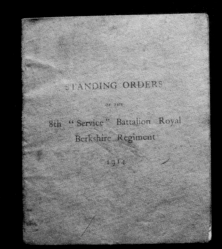

STANDING ORDERS
OF THE
8th "Service" Battalion Royal
Berkshire Regiment
1914

30. *Hair.*—The following K.R. 1696 is published for information and guidance of all ranks. The hair of the head will be kept short. The chin and under-lip will be shaved, but not the upper-lip.
Whiskers if worn will be of moderate length.

In the "on guard" position, the point of the bayonet must threaten the *opponent's throat.* Previous to returning "on guard" a strong withdrawal must be made—it requires considerable effort to withdraw a bayonet which has fixed a bone.

1 Teams for the Officers v Sergeants football match at Boyton Park Camp, November 1914. 2 8th Battalion Royal Berkshire Regiment *Standing Orders* booklet (8 pages long). 3. The last item in the *Standing Orders* - moustaches were compulsory! 4 Item from the Battalion's *Physical Training & Bayonet Fighting* booklet that graphically shows the reality of using a bayonet. 5 The officers of the Battalion in Reading in March 1915 (can you spot the differences compared to the one in May?) 6 'A' Company of the 8th Royal Berkshires - multiply this 4 times to see the size of the battalion. 7. Colonel Walton takes the salute as his men parade through Reading. 8 Some of the men in Sandhill Camp equipped in full marching order with rifles & bayonets fixed, not long before embarkation. 9 Digging trenches on Salisbury Plain. Ronald Brakspear marked X, Louis Klemantaski in centre marked ∴.

Photographs taken while training in Reading & on Salisbury Plain: 1 Pay day with Gordon Paramore & Lionel Edwards at desk in centre. **2** Wilfrid Clarke. **3** Morice Thompson (centre), Harold Cohen (rear right). **4** Donald Stileman. **5** Louis Klemantaski (front left), Aubyn Rouse (rear), Clifford Salman (right). **6** Eric Foot. **7** Harold Keable (left), Will Bissley (centre), Mervyn Pugh (right). **8** Gordon Peacock (behind left hand drums) with Regimental band. **9** Eric Foot practises "first aid" on a barely willing victim. **10** Gordon Peacock on horesback with groom. **11** James Barrow (this photo used to give one of his brothers' grandchildren nightmares as a child due to his fierce expression). **12** Lionel Edwards (on the train) is waved off by his commanding officer Colonel William Walton, with the Colonel's wife Emmy further along the platform, as one of the first trains leaves Warminster Station to transport the Battalion to Southampton ready for embarkation for France.

In the summer of 1915, my Gran, aged 14, visited her father and his battalion in their camp. This is her journal, written in an exercise book accompanied by glued-in photographs of the soldiers in training.

My Summer Holiday, July 27th - Aug 10th

Our holiday at Warminster was one of the nicest, in fact the nicest fortnight we spent. Every morning I used to practise the piano for half an hour or three quarters, and then we "war worked", as we had to get 40 red flags done for the baggage wagons of the regiment before they went off to the front.

The pattern was like this: - [see left] - and the letters were blue, and we put two tapes at the bottom of the seam for the stick to go in. We got them done on Tuesday, the 3rd of August, and the regiment went on Saturday the 7th. One day we got an invitation to go to the camp for dinner so we bicycled out, it is about 4 miles, and we arrived very hot but quite ready for dinner.

After dinner which we had at the Mess we went over the camp and saw the different things such as the Cook House, Stables, and the Stores etc, which was very interesting. After we had finished our round we went down to the ranges and watched the men firing, and as the machine guns had just arrived Mr Glen and Captain Cassels, the machine gun officers explained them to us and they were very interesting. We had to go then as it was getting late but we had tea before leaving.

We went down several times to the camp and sometimes the machine guns were firing, and they were making a most awful noise. The Bomb throwing party were also at work one day, and just as we were moving away one of the bombs, which were "home made", and so not very dangerous, burst in the air and the tin came flying over in our direction and missed me by about half an inch!

One day the 78th Brigade under General Thomas, and also several other Brigades passed through Warminster, and we watched them go through. They took about 2½ hours to go right through, and all the little shop boys were out watching them too so everybody had to bring home their own purchases.

A few days before the regiment left Warminster the officers gave a dinner party to which we were asked also Mrs Bartlett, Miss Carew, and Mrs Gentry-Birch. We had a very nice time and we motored back and we weren't in bed till about quarter to twelve. On Saturday the regiment had to go off to the front, and so as they were going to start at 6.30 and Mrs Bartlett lived so far away she came to stay the night with us

—

Patricia Walton, standing between Charles Bartlett (left) & her father William Walton, along with sister Diana & brother Billy.

A SUMMER HOLIDAY JOURNAL OF 1915

and brought Miss Carew. In the morning we got up at 5.30, and had tea and biscuits and made tea for the officers at the station, and when we were on our way we found out that the first train had gone a minute before, and it was only 6.15. Just then Daddy came along in the General's car and we all packed in & went to the railway bridge where they picked up the wagons but just as Mrs Bartlett got down on to the line, the train went before she could say goodbye to Major Bartlett who was commanding the first train. We then all had to go back again, so as there was hardly an inch of room in the car, I went in Mr Berlein's side car in which he had brought Daddy up in the morning to have some breakfast and a bath. The second train we saw off in plenty of time, and the officers enjoyed the tea very much indeed. Daddy went by the third train, so we came home and had a very large breakfast party of fourteen when we came back, consisting of our party, three officers who had been left behind as surplus and Mrs Hicks, one of the officers' mothers and Mrs Gentry-Birch.

The rest of the day seemed very lonely indeed.

My Gran, Patricia (more usually known as Peg), is of fundamental importance to this project. It was she who showed me her father's letters from the First World War. I have a clear image in my head of that day. I was 16 at the time and what amazes me now, looking back on it, is how I didn't take it any further at the time. Oh, what a project this would be if I'd asked all the right questions then, and written everything down (a common cry from family historians and something that I've been trying to communicate during my visits to schools). It was especially surprising as she had given me an interest in history, and showed me that it was all right to be always asking questions. In the end I was exceptionally lucky that she stayed alive long enough and retained enough memories to answer my questions at the very beginning of my research. This photograph shows her 82 years after writing her 1915 Summer Journal. Her memory was not what it was, but she had not forgotten that summer, and as I read her the names I could see her light up with memories of some, but the darkness of the loss was not far behind.

Mrs Emily Walton

PRESENTED
TO
MRS WALTON
BY THE OFFICERS
OF THE 8TH BATTALION ROYAL BERKSHIRE REGIMENT
TO COMMEMORATE THE PERIOD
FROM WHEN THE
BATTALION WAS RAISED, TO ITS DEPARTURE TO
FRANCE ON ACTIVE SERVICE
OCTOBER 1. 1914 ~ AUGUST 7. 1915.

ROYAL BERKSHIRE REGT
CHINA

MAJOR. C.F.N.BARTLETT	LIEUT. L.H.BERLEIN	2ND LIEUT. T.E.ALLEN
.. R.W.BRAKSPEAR	.. H.K.CASSELS	.. G.F.MARSH
CAPTAIN. L.H.EDWARDS	.. D.C.GLEN	.. T.B.LAWRENCE
.. D.TOSETTI	.. D.F.STILEMAN	.. A.R.ROUSE
.. W.S.D.OLDMAN	.. G.GENTRY BIRCH	.. H.C.L.KEABLE
.. R.M.COOTE	.. B.F.HICKS	.. W.H.BISSLEY
.. C.G.PARAMORE	2ND LIEUT. T.G.ROBINSON	.. C.R.WATSON
.. D.M.HANNA	.. W.G.HOBBS	.. C.A.WILLIAMSON
LIEUT. C.S.CLOAKE	.. W.G.HAYNES	HON. LIEUT. & QRMR J.BARROW
.. T.G.PEACOCK	.. C.S.PARTALI	

Before they left for France, the officers of the battalion presented a silver tray to their Commanding Officer's wife. This was the sort of gesture that fell in with the traditions of the Regular Army, each battalion of which had its regimental silver. It is difficult in a photograph this size to show just how substantial an item it is, but suffice to say that it is 4 kg of solid silver and at 69 x 43 cm is bigger than the top of my filing cabinet.

Mrs Walton arranged the engraving, including on the back of the tray the names of the officers who had been selected to accompany William Walton into action. Many of those in the Group Photograph were left in reserve as future reinforcements, and the 29 listed here (including 3 who were away when the Group Photograph was taken) must have been his top picks to lead his men. Within 10 weeks of this tray being presented, half of them were dead.

Embarkation & Battle Preparation

Right up to the time of their embarkation, the men were in the dark as to their destination. There were rumours of Egypt, but in the end the 8th Royal Berkshires disembarked in Le Havre on 8th August 1915. They were soon on a train to a camp near St Omer where they spent a week familiarising themselves with the rifles with which they had just been issued. Daily marches then took them towards the front, where they had their first experience of the front line trenches, each company piggy-backing on a different battalion in the line who showed them the ropes. They spent some time in support trenches towards the end of August but for the most part it was a case of training and more training. This poem was amongst Hugh Cassels' effects and tells of this time:

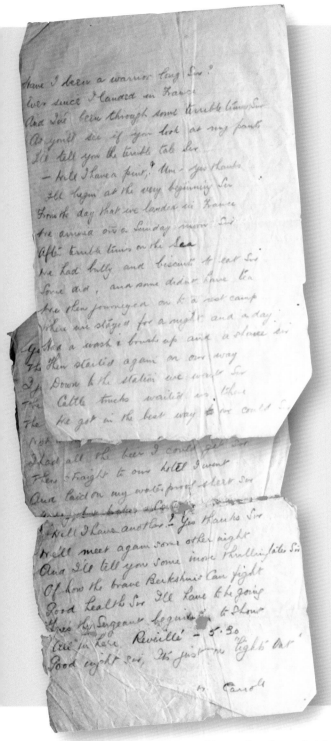

Have I been a warrior long Sir?

Have I been a warrior long Sir?
Ever since I landed in France
And I've been through some terrible times Sir
As you'll see if you look at my pants
I'll tell you the terrible tale Sir
- Will I have pint? Um – yes thanks
I'll begin at the very beginning Sir
From the day that we landed in France
we arrived on a Sunday morn Sir
After terrible times on the Sea
We had bully and biscuits to eat Sir
Some did, and some didn't have tea
We then journeyed on to a camp
Where we stayed for a night and a day
Had a wash & brush up and a shave Sir
Then started again on our way
Down to the station we went Sir
Cattle trucks waited us there
We got in the best way we could Sir
There wasn't much room for to spare
For two days we travelled along Sir
Our journey then came to an end
And we all toddled out of the station
Another brief rest for to spend
It was then that we had our first pay day
My word what a day for the boys
We all had a few pints apiece Sir
But they soon put an end to our joys
We were ordered to start once again Sir
On a Sunday all merry and Bright
We done about 10 or 12 miles Sir
Then we put up again for the night
Away we started next day Sir
Away to our next resting camp
Consisting of one or two "boozers"
And a place that is called the "Red Lamp"
We rested again for a time Sir
Then started away for the trenches

And the day before we got there Sir
The rain had been falling in drenches
We waded our way through the water
You ought to have seen us, 'twas fine
And a few miles brought us to the end Sir
Smash bang, in the front firing line
Two days and two nights were we there Sir
And not one of our men did we lose
Perhaps the Germans knew who was there Sir
And were having a time on the booze
At last up came our relief Sir
And back very soon we made tracks
Not exactly like two year olds Sir
For just feel the weight of our packs
Back down the road then we galloped
On horses? Sir no on our feet
You've not seen the 8th R Berks march Sir?
My word, then, you have missed a treat
We got back to our Billets again Sir
Back to our old resting camp
You know the place that I mean Sir
The place where they've got the "Red Lamp"
I just got a couple of pints Sir
The Red Lamp was full to the hilt
The Boys of the Village were there Sir
Not to mention the lads in the Kilt
I had all the beer I could get Sir
Then straight to our hotel I went
And laid on my waterproof sheet Sir
Happy, flat broke and content
Will I have another? Yes thanks Sir
We'll meet again some other night
And I'll tell you some more thrilling tales Sir
Of how the brave Berkshires can fight
Good health Sir I'll have to be going
Here's the Sergeant beginning to shout
All in here, Reveillé – 5.30
Good night Sir, it's just in "lights out"

Written in Hugh's hand, the poet is named as 'W Carroll'. The only W Carroll in the 8th Royal Berkshires was Private William Carroll, 11543. He was killed on the first day at Loos and has no known grave.

At the beginning of September they still did not know of the bigger plans for them, though Colonel Walton thought *"there may be a push over here before long"*. In the meantime, the training continued, as he wrote to his wife:

'Many of the officers of battalions out here now have a military education that begins and ends in trench warfare. If we had to do any other fighting in the open they & their men would soon be in confusion - they say so themselves. They could not put out an advance guard & if they were put out they would hardly know what to do. But from practice they know all about trench warfare. Now we are picking up all they can tell us about trench war, & if it came to fighting in the open we should not be in any difficulty. All we want is a little more practice under fire. But in the meanwhile we are practising hard at all the things which we have been told about. Today I found a suitable place for digging some trenches & also some old trenches which were dug about a year ago which fit in to my digging & make a position which will be perfectly splendid for practising the attack & defence. It was great luck finding the old trenches & being able to make use of them in this way. Everyone is working hard trying to complete our education.'

By 11th September, they were practising the attack in earnest, and Colonel Walton *"went with the General & other C.O.s to the trenches & had a good look at the German trenches – Such a lot of wire entanglement miles & miles of it. It would take a long time to get through even if there were no enemy – I think they must have seen us looking at them as they shelled us & about half a dozen 4 or 5 inch shells came much nearer than I liked – one about 10 yards off. The noise they make as they are coming is extraordinary you can hear them & tell if they are coming near or not, & when they do come near you wish you were the size of a mouse & could get well down a deep hole. I can't say I enjoy being shelled a bit. One feels much the same as when one has had a narrow shave of being run over by a motor. But I believe one gets used to it after a bit."*

Their strenuous training and preparations continued throughout September, and included an introduction to the procedures required for the release of chlorine gas as part of the assault, and pro-viding fatigue parties to carry the gas cylinders into the front line. An air photo of the German lines enabled them to mock up the trenches they were about to attack, and they used these to practise the assault for a week before the battle.

On 21st September they marched towards the front and bivouacked in a wood where at 6 p.m. Colonel Walton read the Battalion Operation Orders for the attack to all the officers. At 7 p.m. on 23rd September they moved into the front line trenches. A year from their formation, the 8th Royal Berkshires were ready to go into action for the first time.

Cecil Cloake's map: the red lines are German trenches. The 8th Royal Berkshires attacked from left to right towards Hulluch.

The Battle of Loos

At 5.50 a.m. on Saturday 25th September 1915 the British artillery opened their intensive bombardment of the German lines, and simultaneously the gas cylinders were opened to release the chlorine towards the Germans. This first use of gas by the British was not successful. Any wind there was changed direction and the gas settled amongst the men of the 8th Royal Berkshires. Their rudimentary "smoke helmets" provided little protection and soon some of the men were foaming at the mouth as the chlorine settled in the bottom of the trenches. Smoke bombs were thrown out from the front line and this, along with the gas, entirely hid their initial advance from the Germans. As Colonel Walton recalled after the War:

'At 6.30 a.m. on the 25th I had ordered the bugle to sound the advance but the bugler was brought down wounded and his bugle torn by shell fire. I went up to see the men go over and was met by a rush of men coming down the trench to escape our gas. I struggled with them for a bit and thinking example better than precept got out and advanced and they followed me.

As my dugout was on the left of the front trench of the battalion my advance with the men with me was on the left of the battalion and we were in touch with the right of the 2nd Gordons. Owing to the smoke I did not know what was happening to the rest of the battalion. When we got about half a mile from Hulluch and were on the Hulluch road and the smoke having cleared I left the Gordons on my left entrenching themselves on the north of the road as they were held up as we were by our own artillery fire. I moved to the right to find the rest of my men, and eventually collected 180 in the communication trench and blocked it and converted it into a fire trench. No other officer was there except myself. All my staff officers and men were casualties. I may say that during this advance my men and the 2nd Gordons on our left took a party of about 50 German prisoners. I shot two Germans with my revolver as we bumped them at close range owing to the smoke.'

The smoke, whilst shielding them from view, afforded no protection from shrapnel and bullets and many of the casualties came as German artillery and machine-guns fired on No-Man's Land where the 8th Royal Berkshires were advancing and attempting to cut their way through the almost intact German barbed wire. Their first casualties stoked a blood lust in many that did not need much stirring after all the newspaper reports of German atrocities, and by 8 a.m. they had reached Gun Trench (marked in blue biro on the right hand side of Cecil Cloake's map), 1200 yards from their start point. In many cases, the Germans had turned and run, and even with the chaos caused by limited visibility and the many casualties, the battalion kept moving forward, capturing 2 field guns and reaching the German 4th line just in front of Hulluch. Scouting parties were sent to reconnoitre the village but owing to lack of numbers and the flimsiness of the trenches in the face of German counterattacks, Colonel Walton decided to pull back and consolidate in Gun Trench whilst awaiting reinforcements. Colonel Walton was by this time suffering from the effects of gas, and at 10 p.m. he was sent to the rear by the Regimental Medical Officer for medical attention leaving what was left of the Battalion in the command of 20 year old Second Lieutenant Thomas Lawrence, who only a few months before had been a private.

The following morning at 10 a.m. Colonel Walton rejoined his men in the trenches opposite Hulluch. The next two days were spent holding the line and trying to stave off hunger, thirst and tiredness (they ate half their iron ration at noon on the 26th and at that point had no water left). Then on 28th September there is this entry in the Battalion's war diary: '9.0 a.m. The Commanding Officer – Col. W.C. Walton – having received his orders left the trench to proceed to ADEN on duty, where he was to take over the command of a Mobile Force.' This had not come out of the blue. William Walton had been stalling his official employers, the India Office, since receiving these orders in early September, writing to his wife, 'It seems decreed that I am to train battalions but not to lead them into the fight.' But now he could put them off no longer. What came next in the war diary is extraordinary, given the dispassionate nature of most war diary entries and the renowned stiff upper lip conventions of the day:

'It was not without tears in his eyes that he said goodbye to his Officers and one could see that it hurt him greatly to leave his Battalion especially under such conditions and at such a time.'

Reading this called to mind my Gran saying how her father loved his soldiers more than his own family, and brought home how much he must have suffered in seeing the Battalion that he had raised from nothing and trained over the course of a year effectively destroyed in a morning. Below is the letter he wrote to his wife. It was this letter that my Gran showed me all those years before. It was its rediscovery which started me looking into his history and then led me to find the Group Photograph, and it was the reading of the 'tears in his eyes' that set the seal for me not to let go of this project until it was finished. There has been so much else in this project but that is a crystalline moment that I will never forget.

My Dearest
Just a line to say that I hope to follow this at the very shortest possible space. To go to Aden to take up Command of the Mobile Column there – Thank God I have been spared without a scratch after taking part in the greatest fight in history. Since Saturday 25th at 5.30 A.M. I have been in the firing line – at the very forefront and am of course dog tired as they ought to have relieved us earlier, but I was quite happy in my Regiment which did grandly and earned high praise – The losses very severe – I took in 20 officers & about 900 men & the remaining effective strength when I left them at 9 A.M. today was myself & 2 other officers & 220 men – All the rest were killed wounded or missing – I hope many may still turn up. Peacock, Hicks, Berlein & Cassels and perhaps Keable all reported killed, remainder only wounded I hope. I kept Major Bartlett, Capt Edwards, Capt Coote, Mr Robinson, Mr Cloake + Mr Spartali in reserve so they are now available & have joined since the first fight. I have handed over command to Major B but am sorry to say I left him looking poorly & he had got lumbago badly. The battle was at an extremely interesting stage when I left – the great fear I had was that our reserves may be insufficient, but in fighting spirit we are undefeated and must be victorious please God. Major Brakspear & Tosetti are not badly wounded I hear & many wounds are not severe
your loving Husband
Am just going to get ticket + collect kit – Hope arrive tomorrow 29th

Despite his phlegmatic summing up of the casualties and his hopes that 'many may still turn up', it was not to be, as you can see from the pictures on the right. The 8th Royal Berkshires were relieved at 11 a.m. on 28th September. Major Bartlett did take over as Commanding Officer and they were soon in action again in an attack on 13th October that was doomed from the start and saw additional severe losses for not an iota of gain.

1

7th August 1915, embarkation: ■ named on the silver tray, ■ Harold Cohen had died of illness in Reading on 18th July 1915.

2

25th September 1915, after 1st attack at Loos: ■ dead ■ wounded or gassed ■ others from silver tray still active with Battalion.

3

13th October 1915, after 2nd attack at Loos: ■ dead ■ wounded or gassed ■ others from silver tray still fit & active with Battalion.

4

11th November 1918, end of the War: ■ dead ■ seriously wounded during the War ■ seriously ill during the War. None of these men was serving with the 8th Battalion Royal Berkshire Regiment when the War ended.

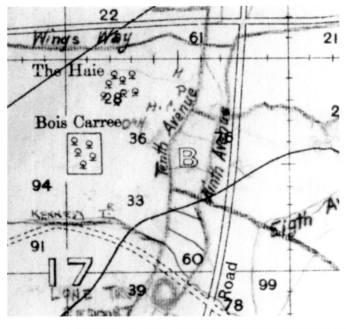

Bois-Carré Military Cemetery, Haisnes (above) is on the site of what was originally a small copse, the remains of which hid the German machine-guns that caused so many casualties on the first day at Loos. Note the completely flat landscape - any cover outside of the trenches can have only come from smoke and gas and shell holes. The precisely cut grass and uniform white headstones belie the horrific ugly slaughter that was in this place.

This map shows burials on the battlefield in the area of Bois Carré - the pencilled initials were written by Cecil Cloake and signify: G17b.3.7 Oldman & Haynes, G17b.5.9 Hicks, G17b.5.8½ Peacock, G17b.5.7½ Hobbs & Cassels.

Hugh Cassels, Wilfrid Oldman & Billy Haynes (not present for the Group Photograph) are buried at Bois-Carré along with Harold Keable. Basil Hicks is buried at Dud Corner. Three more years of war in this area and delays due to the enormous numbers of bodies to process meant that the graves of Gordon Peacock & Tod Hobbs were lost and their bodies never identified. They are named on the Loos Memorial to the Missing at Dud Corner.

It has been said that in the nearly 4 years between the settling of the Front into lines of trenches and the Hundred Days Offensive at the End of the War, the British Army achieved only two breaks of the German lines. One of these was with the use of tanks at Cambrai in November 1917, and the other was by the 8th Royal Berkshires during the Battle of Loos - a battalion that had only received its rifles and machine-guns two months before going into action. In the end, though, it was for nothing - the reserves could not be brought up in time, and the Battle of Loos petered out in dismal failure. It may not have been what William Walton termed *'the greatest fight in history'*, but with 75,000 British infantry making the initial attack it can lay claim to being the biggest battle that the British Army had fought in its history up until that time. As a comparison, the Battle of Waterloo 100 years before had involved 25,000 British troops. And the number of the casualties was also on a previously unknown scale. Cecil Cloake later wrote, '*More British soldiers were killed on the first morning of the Battle of Loos than died on both sides in all three services on the whole of D-Day 1944*'. It says something about the awful magnitude of what happened in the following years on the Somme and at Passchendaele that the Battle of Loos has largely been forgotten.

It is also easy to forget that in amongst all these big numbers and statistics are individual human beings whose loss tore at the insides of their loved ones leaving wounds that stayed with them until the days that they died. Elizabeth Berlein was the mother of Leslie Berlein, who was killed at Loos. Her eldest son Charlie had been killed near Ypres only 3 months before. In her grief she wrote this poem:

I shall lie quiet, quiet
On either hand a son,
And wait in timeless patience
Till time's long night be done.
As in the days of living
They'll lie close by my side,
And time shall be forgotten
And space, wherein they died.
And in the sightless darkness
My yearning hands shall reach
To make sure of their nearness,
And take my love to each.
I shall not draw them closer
Nor stir their slumber deep,
For fear a flash of memory
Might stab the dark of sleep.
I shall lie quiet, quiet
One knowledge in my breast,
That close beside me, sleeping
Lie my two sons, at rest.

1 View from Bois-Carré Military Cemetery of the Double Crassier, slag heaps that are a reminder that this is a mining area. They are the most prominent features of the local landscape in 2015 just as they were in 1915, when they were christened the "Twa Bings" by soldiers of the Black Watch (for those not familiar with Scottish vernacular they are referring to two prominent female features). **2** Dud Corner Cemetery at Loos. 5 of the men from the Group Photograph are buried here, and 6 others are amongst over 20,000 names on the Loos Memorial to the Missing which is on the walls of the cemetery.

THE MEN

For some, the Battle of Loos was their end.
For others, it was just the beginning of their suffering.
For all, the Great War changed everything.

These are their stories.

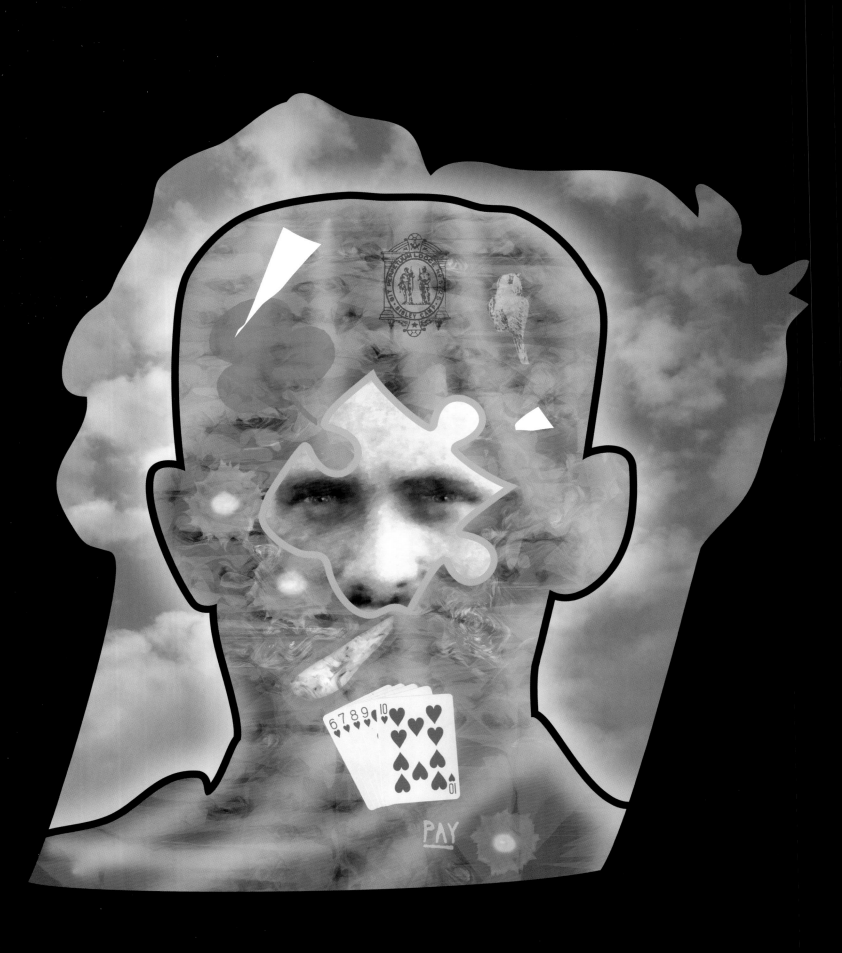

children
grandchildren
great-grandchildren
great-great-grandchildren
great-great-great-grandchildren

2nd Lieutenant **Thomas Edward 'Tom' 'Ted' ALLEN** later Lieutenant

b. Tuesday 17th November 1891 in Kiltegan, near Baltinglass, Co Wicklow, Ireland
d. Sunday 11th January 1959 in Edgware, Middlesex, England (heart attack)
Time on Earth: 67 years, 1 month, 26 days
Cremated, ashes scattered, no known memorial

1830	1840	1850	1860	1870	1880	1890	1900	1910	1920	1930	1940	1950	1960	1970	1980	1990	2000	2010	

Lost his father very early and had to take responsibility for his family. Moved to England and passed top in the UK Civil Service exam. Shot in the right bicep, right chest and left thigh, bayoneted in the right side of his abdomen, and gassed, he survived a night in the open after the first day at Loos. By 1917 he was fit enough to go on a tour to the USA to promote War Bonds. On the ship returning, he won heavily at cards but knowing that the losers could ill afford their loss he stayed up all night until he'd lost it all back to them. Retired as Senior Tax Inspector for London. A larger than life Irishman, hospitable and a good raconteur, he could also be irascible (probably due to pain from his wounds) and went spare when his son suggested joining the Army.

Stained glass window: One of his expressions was *"Let's fry the canary"* which translated as *"We may not have much, but let's push the boat out"*.

—

1 Parents Robert & Frances. **2/3** With wife Mick & son Brian. **4/5** Great-grandchildren Daniel & Greta.

1

2 ‹‹‹

3

4 ‹‹‹

5

2ND LIEUT. T.E. ALLEN

J. BARROW   LIEUT.

HON. LIEUT & Q⁵ᵐᴿ J. BARROW

James Barrow.

LIEUTENANT & QMR.
J. BARROW
ROYAL BERKSHIRE REGIMENT
1ST JUNE 1916 AGE 47.

Q. M. & HON. LIEUT. JAMES BARROW. ROYAL BERKSHIRE REG.

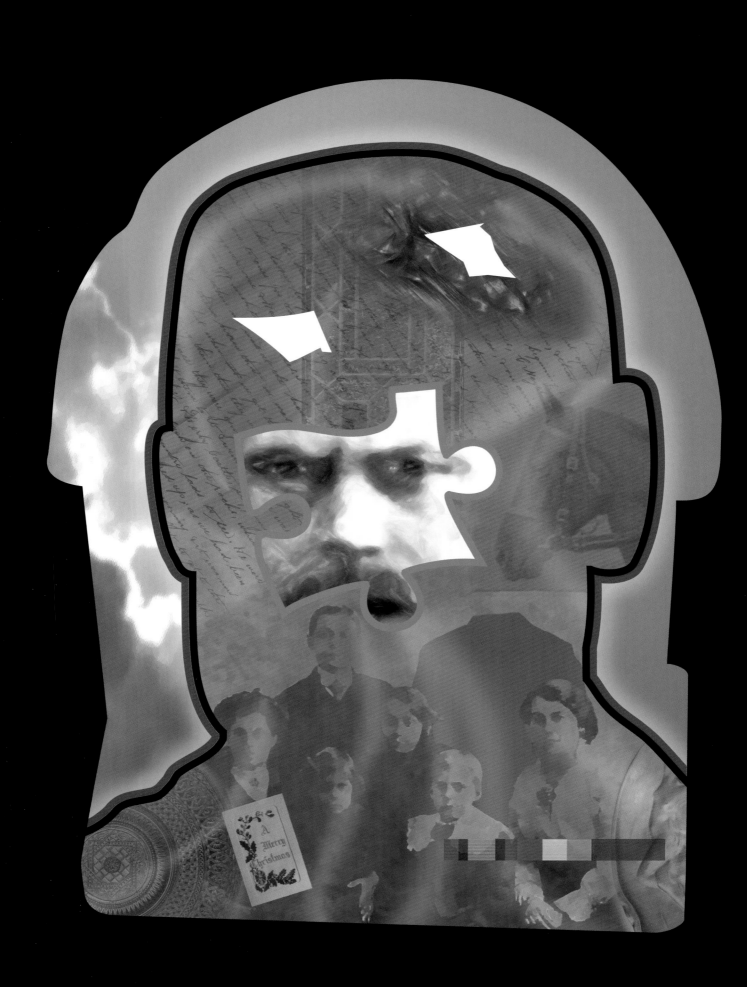

children
grandchildren
great-grandchildren
great-great-grandchildren
great-great-great-grandchildren

Honorary Lieutenant & Quartermaster # James 'Jim' BARROW

b. Monday 27th July 1868 in Culcheth, Lancashire, England
d. Thursday 1st June 1916 in 47 Auxiliary Hospital, Bully-les-Mines, Pas-de-Calais, France
(of wounds received at 9.30 pm when hit by a shell whilst with a party delivering rations to the trenches)
Time on Earth: 47 years, 10 months, 6 days — Buried, CWGC gravestone, 2 known memorials

1830 1840 1850 1860 1870 1880 1890 1900 1910 1920 1930 1940 1950 1960 1970 1980 1990 2000 2010

After retiring from a full career in the Army Pay Corps, he was working as a docker to keep his young family when war broke out. His wife was furious with him for joining up immediately and never visited his grave after the War, living on for 35 years as a widow. Only one branch from his 5 siblings and his 5 children produced offspring who are still living, and all 3 of his great-grandchildren work in education – apt because it was education that enabled him to make his way in the world from humble beginnings (a beautifully handwritten and eloquent account of a holiday to the Isle of Man when he was 18 is testament to the quality of his schooling).

Stained glass window: The Christmas Card was in a suitcase of his family's belongings that was in the possession of a woman who as a girl had been taken in by his daughter Elsie (and who later went on to be a dancer on the Morecambe & Wise Show).

—

1 Certificate from his school in 1879. **2** Behind his wife Alice & children George & Amy, in Cape Town during Boer War. **3** Son George, became a POW in 1918. **4** Youngest children Ethel, James & Elsie. **5** Widow Alice in the 1940s.

children
grandchildren
great-grandchildren
great-great-grandchildren
great-great-great-grandchildren

Major **Charles Frederick Napier Bartlett** later Lieutenant Colonel

b. Friday 12th April 1878 in Stone, Buckinghamshire, England
d. Saturday 28th December 1940 in Putney, Surrey, England (gangrene in leg artery resulting in amputation, pneumonia)
Time on Earth: 62 years, 8 months, 17 days
Cremated, ashes scattered, no known memorial

1830 1840 1850 1860 1870 1880 1890 1900 1910 1920 1930 1940 1950 1960 1970 1980 1990 2000 2010

My great-grandfather's second-in-command who later took over command of the battalion, including leading them during the Battle of the Somme. After a long search via Johannesburg & Shropshire I found his granddaughter in London. She said she had a few of his letters. "A few" turned out to be 341, written to his wife between August 1915 and March 1917. They chart his journey from bluff optimism to ground-down exhaustion and are the most incredible mix of military administration and horror, gossip and Wodehouseian antics, invariably signed off *"Thine, Charles"*. A bon viveur, regarded by his wider family as a black sheep (he and his wife were divorced after the War), he also had a kindness and sense of duty to his fellow man and lives on in these letters.

Stained glass window: An excerpt from a typical letter: *"Poor Colonel Graeme commanding the Camerons was killed yesterday by a big shell which just happened to land plumb in the trench, as he was walking back from our headquarters to his. The Doctor who was with him was blown some distance along the trench, but otherwise than being much shaken was untouched. The kippers have arrived & were excellent eating, for which many many thanks".*

—

1 As a young man. **2** 3rd from left with his wife Peggy & other officers on leave in Nice, 1916. **3** Wife Peggy. **4** The end of a letter from 8th April 1916: *"Thine in haste, Charles x this flourish is owing to a shell coming too close."*

1

2

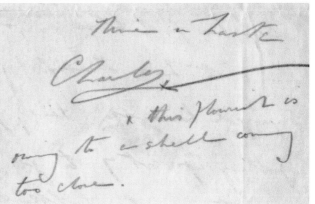

3 ‹‹‹

4

MAJOR C.F.N.BARTLETT

L. H. BERLEIN

L.H.BERLEIN,

L. H. BERLEIN

Berlein . L . H.   Lt . R . Berks . Regt.
                    1915
France 1915

BERLEIN. L. H.   LT LESLIE H. BERLEIN 8 R. BERKS R.

BERLEIN, L.H. ROYAL BERKS. REGT.   Leslie Herman Berlein

Leslie Berlein   LIEUT. L.H. BERLEIN

                    L. H. BERLEIN

LIEUTENANT
L. H. BERLEIN
ROYAL BERKSHIRE REGIMENT
25TH SEPTEMBER 1915 AGE 22

THE SOULS OF THE RIGHTEOUS
ARE IN THE HAND OF GOD

children
grandchildren
great-grandchildren
great-great-grandchildren
great-great-great-grandchildren

Lieutenant **Leslie Herman BERLEIN**

b. Monday 30th January 1893 in Doornfontein, Johannesburg, Transvaal, South Africa
d. Saturday 25th September 1915, near Hulluch, Pas-de-Calais, France (killed in action on the first day of the Battle of Loos)
Time on earth: 22 years, 7 months, 27 days
Buried, CWGC gravestone, 10 known memorials, also a wooden cross in his nephew's garden which succumbed to the environment

1830 1840 1850 1860 1870 1880 1890 1900 1910 1920 1930 1940 1950 1960 1970 1980 1990 2000 2010

The son of a tough German Jew and a sensitive and intelligent Irish Catholic. His father made his fortune in South African mining, and was an Anglophile who became a British citizen and sent his children to English public schools. After losing 2 sons in the War, though, he returned to South Africa and never opened the boxes containing his sons' medals, as well as directing that the trunks of his sons' belongings should be passed down through the generations. Leslie was a fun-loving and lovely non-conformist - he and his brothers would blow their whole term's pocket money on champagne when they got on the train to go back to school, and he stands out as different in nearly every group photograph he's in. Beloved by his men, his body was found surrounded by them. His

memory was fully kept alive by his sister Renée who was 14 when he died and lived to be 97.

Stained glass window: The fish is part of an illustration from *The Water Babies* by Charles Kingsley. The picture was a great favourite of Leslie's.

---

1 Father Julius. **2** Mother Elizabeth. **3** Brother Charlie, killed near Ypres in 1915. **4** Brother Walter "Bubbles". **5** Sister Renée, just before the War. **6** Renée in the 1980s.

1
2 «‹‹
3

4
5 «‹‹
6

The two trunks contain all of the belongings of Leslie & his brother Charlie at the time that they were killed in the War. Here is the list of their contents as written by their father Julius:

2 Packets of coat buttons, Pouch with scissors & bell hooks, Pocket Ambulance case, Toothbrush in celluloid case, Lead pencil & compass, Box of sundries including silver matchbox, Housewife, 2 Water bottles (Khaki covered), Field glasses in case, Mess tin, Revolver in holster, Knapsack, Books (Sinister Street Vol 2, Minnie's Bishop), 2 Map cases, Wire cutters, Combination pocket knife, Field dressing, Shaving mirror, Leather box, 2 Pouches, Sword frog, Writing case, Packet of coat buttons, Silk handkerchief, Silk scarf, 2 metal flasks, Electric torch, 2 Sam Browne belts, Cooking tin, 4 Military maps, Note book, Order & Memo book, Packet of letters, Tobacco pouch, Cigarette case etc, 2 Letter cases, Field Message book, 2 Water pillows, Map case with field service pocket book, Combination knife fork & spoon, Cooking utensils, Small notebook, 2 Swords, 2 Walking sticks, Small leather pocket, 1 Pair shoes, Haversack.

Other items I found were:
Various pieces of household silver, Packs of cards, Dance cards marked up with partners danced with, Fold-up lantern still with the soot on it from when it was last used, Cigarette lighter engraved "Leslie, January 30 1914" (his 21st birthday), Swagger sticks, Leather gaiters, Photographs of family & school & university & their house in Berkhamsted, Charlie's diary from 1910, Postcards from visits to Germany, First World War uniform identification guide, 8th Royal Berkshire Regiment *Standing Orders* and *Physical Training & Bayonet Fighting* booklets, Notes about a Battalion sports day, Messages written between the officers.

The 2 swords and the revolver were stolen in a burglary in South Africa. Many years later, I received an email from a chap in the USA who was negotiating to buy a Colt revolver engraved "8th RBR, Lt L H Berlein" and in looking online had found my Group Photograph website. Needless to say he wasn't exactly thrilled to find that it was hot and I do not know its current whereabouts.

1 He looks elsewhere. 2 21st birthday party in his rooms in Cambridge (3rd from right), 1914. 3 Providing an attraction on Hunstanton Pier just before the War. 4 My Gran remembered that he *"found military discipline difficult"*. 5 Leslie in the centre of his platoon. 6 His spirit lives on in great great nephew Steph.

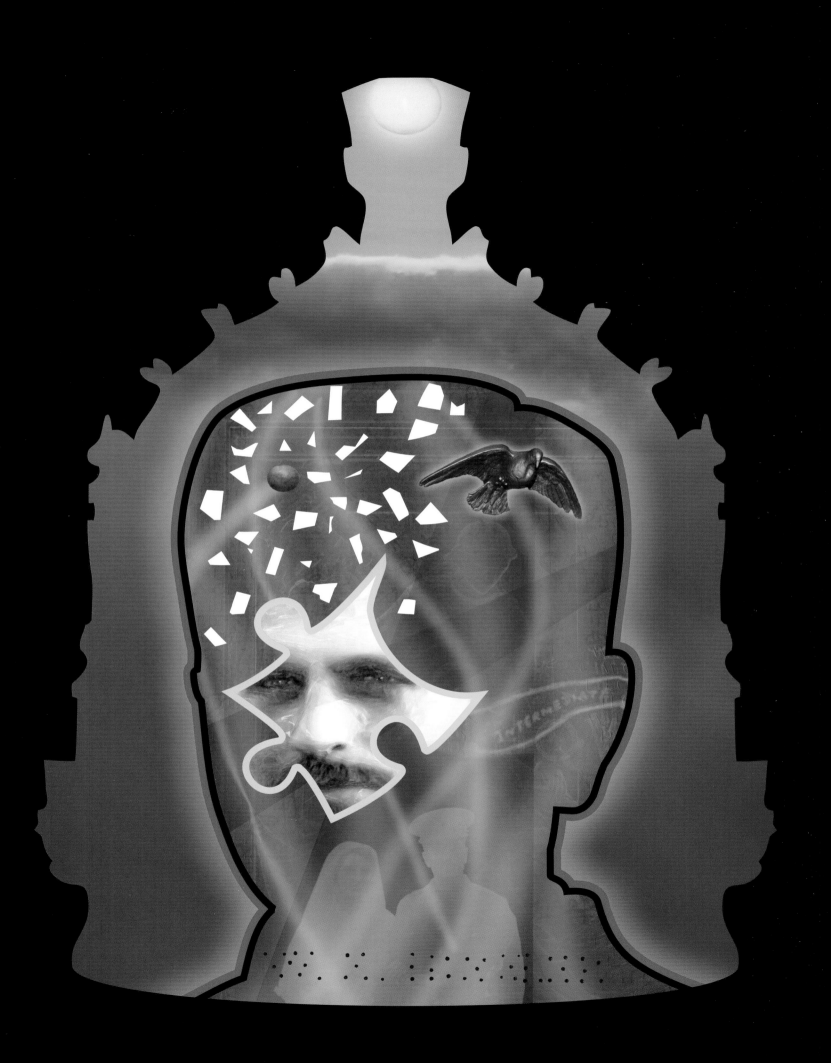

children
grandchildren
great-grandchildren
great-great-grandchildren
great-great-great-grandchildren

2nd Lieutenant **William Howe 'Will' BISSLEY**

b. Monday 9th July 1888 in Boyn Hill, Maidenhead, Berkshire, England
d. on the afternoon of Friday 18th August 1916, in the area of the Intermediate Line near Bazentin-le-Petit, Somme, France
(killed in action in an attack during the Battle of the Somme)
Time on Earth: 28 years, 1 month, 10 days — Body never found, no known grave, 12 known memorials

1830 1840 1850 1860 1870 1880 1890 1900 1910 1920 1930 1940 1950 1960 1970 1980 1990 2000 2010

When war broke out, he was working as a teacher in London whilst in the final year of his degree at the London School of Economics (determined to be in the best position to provide for his future wife, a girl he had loved since they had both set eyes on each other as children in the church choir). He went to France with the 8th Royal Berkshires in August 1915, but didn't go into action with them at Loos as he had been appointed brigade bombing officer (there is a photograph of him with one of the cricket ball grenades used in bombing – no doubt his abilities as a star local cricketer in Maidenhead stood him in good stead). He married in December 1915 and had a 2 day honeymoon in Torquay before he returned to the front. His wife had only seen him once more for a short leave, when in August 1916 she had a premonition that he had died. She went into labour and their daughter was born 4 days after he was killed on the Somme (possibly by his own artillery, one gun of which was dropping short into the 8th Royal Berkshires). From the narrow thread of his short marriage have grown the lives of 4 grandchildren, 8 great grandchildren, and 14 great great grandchildren, including the latest, who was born in March 2015 and christened William John Howe.

Stained glass window: The red stripes are taken from a photograph of the red carpet going down the aisle of the church in which he and his bride worshipped and were married. The outside frame shape and the dove are from the ornately carved and gilded font cover that the family commissioned as a memorial to him.

—

1 Mother Elizabeth. **2** Will as a boy. **3** Wife-to-be Muriel. **4** Father Frank in the centre with the workforce of his building company.

1
—

2 ‹‹‹
—

3
—

4
—

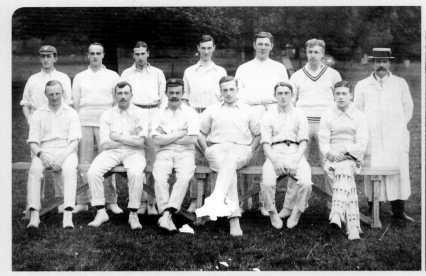

His fiancée Mu's engagement ring. Will & Mu rode their bicycles to Maidenhead Thicket, a bold adventure when young ladies were supposed to be chaperoned at all times in the company of men. Will had brought with him a selection of rings, on loan from a friend whose father ran the local jeweller's. Mu made her choice and he took the rest back. She wore it for the next 67 years.

1 Seated 4th from left. This picture is still up on display at Boyne Hill Cricket Club. **2** Between Williamson & Keable whilst training. **3** Will & Mu's wedding on 8th December 1915.

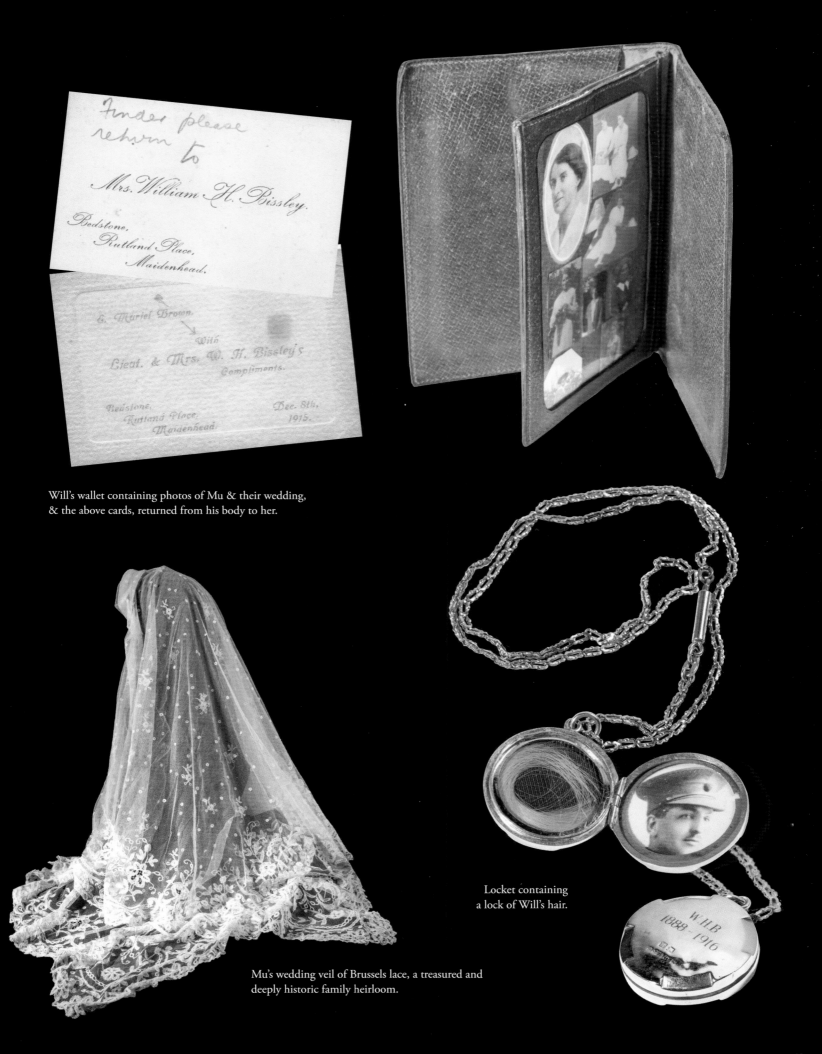

Finder please return to
Mrs. William H. Bissley.
Bedstone,
Rutland Place,
Maidenhead.

G. Muriel Brown.
With
Lieut. & Mrs. W. H. Bissley's
Compliments.

Bedstone,
Rutland Place,
Maidenhead.

Dec. 8th,
1915.

Will's wallet containing photos of Mu & their wedding, & the above cards, returned from his body to her.

Mu's wedding veil of Brussels lace, a treasured and deeply historic family heirloom.

Locket containing a lock of Will's hair.

WHB
1888 - 1916

1 Widow Mu holds their daughter Betty. **2** A beautiful & apt memorial to William Bissley in All Saints Church, Maidenhead, Berkshire. **3** Daughter Betty's wedding wearing her mother's bridal veil, as Mu beams with joy on the left. **4** Mu's 90th birthday party, with Betty behind and all the next generations around her. **5** Mu re-joined her Will in 1982. **6** The family in 2009 - from the briefest of marriages to the fullness of life.

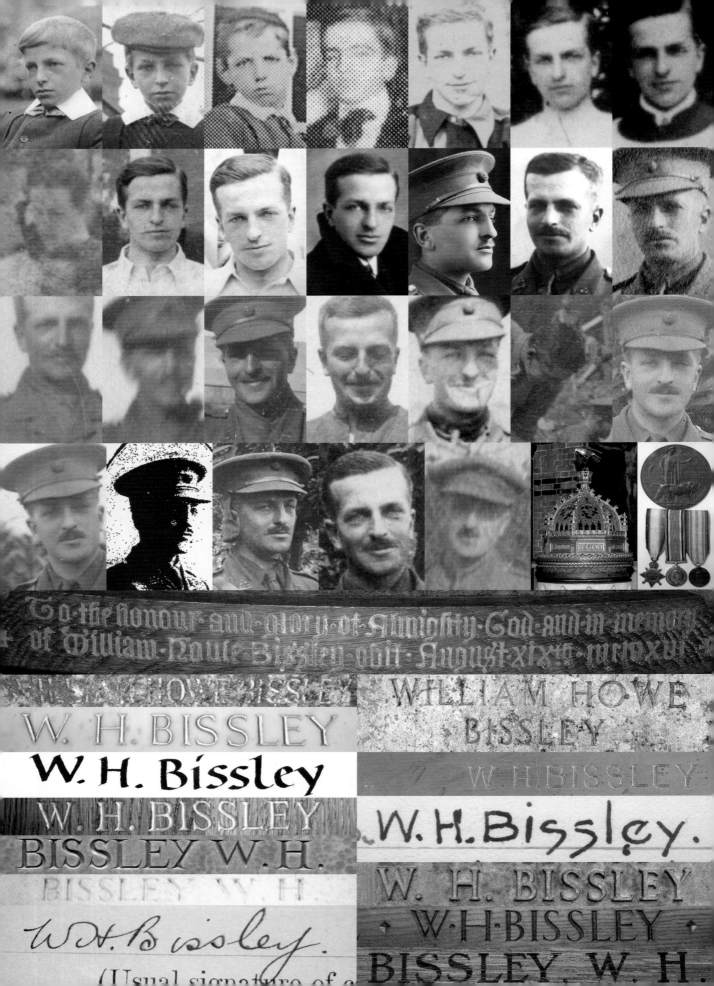

To the honour and glory of Almighty God and in memory
of William Howe Bissley obit August XIXth MCMXVI

WILLIAM HOWE BISSLEY

WILLIAM HOWE BISSLEY

W. H. BISSLEY

W. H. Bissley

W. H. BISSLEY

W. H. BISSLEY

W. H. Bissley.

BISSLEY W. H.

BISSLEY W. H.

W. H. BISSLEY

W. H. BISSLEY

W. H. Bissley.

BISSLEY. W. H.

(Usual signature of

Geoffrey. H. Black.
(late Royal Berks

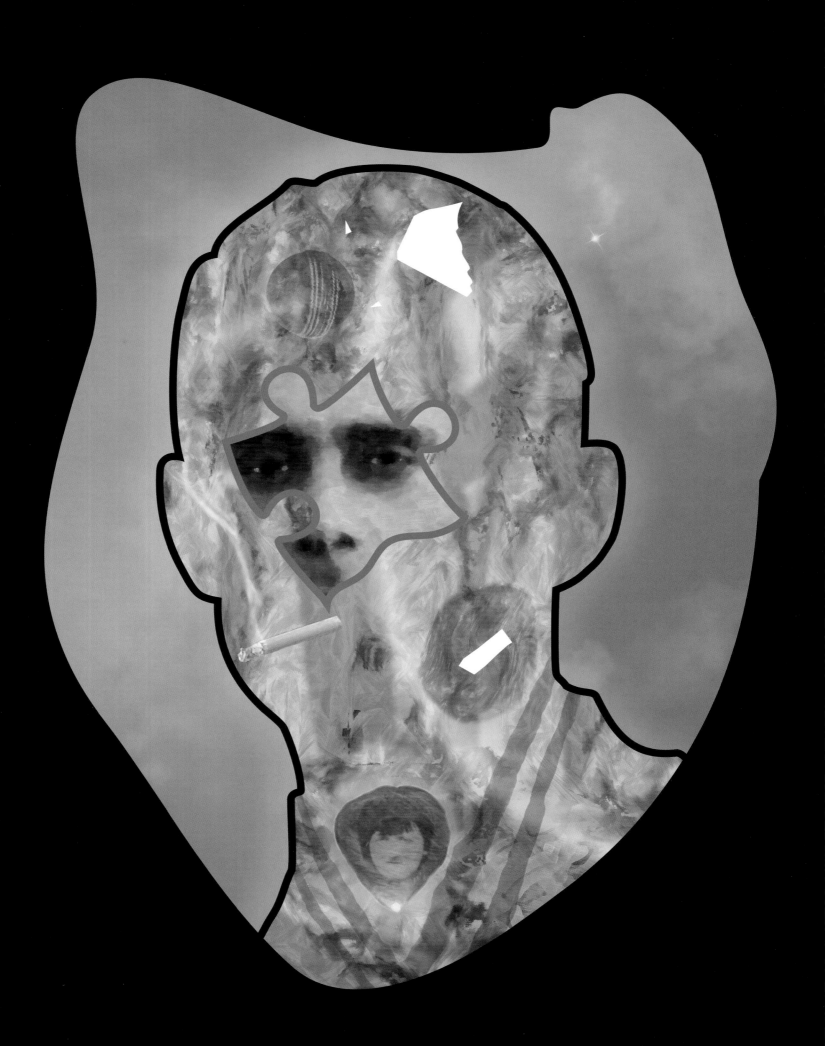

children —————————
grandchildren —————————
great-grandchildren —————————
great-great-grandchildren —————————
great-great-great-grandchildren —————————

2nd Lieutenant **Geoffrey Heslop BLACK** later Lieutenant

b. Sunday 26th January 1896 in Bescot, Walsall, Warwickshire, England
d. Wednesday 29th May 1946 in Stapleton, Bristol, Gloucestershire, England (tuberculosis)
Time on Earth: 50 years, 4 months, 4 days
Cremated, ashes scattered, no known memorial

1830   1840   1850   1860   1870   1880   1890   1900   1910   1920   1930   1940   1950   1960   1970   1980   1990   2000   2010

It's amazing to think that after all the bloody destruction experienced by these men, the only physical evidence is a not very clear photograph taken after a day's cricket in the 1930s that shows the scar on Geoffrey Black's neck from a shrapnel wound received in 1916. The civil service opportunity he had before the War was no longer available when he demobilised, and he never really settled into the career his father thought was his due. Though he died young, 55 years later he was remembered with great warmth by his wife's niece (who was also very kind to me – on hearing I was ill she sent me a cheque with instructions to buy a bottle of brandy).

Stained glass window: When his wife-to-be met him she was set on getting him even though he was engaged to his landlord's daughter with whom he was about to go on holiday. He felt honour bound to go on the holiday but was made to promise to write to her every day. "He came back unsoiled and then they married and were happy".

—

1 The scar in the 1930s. **2** In Dean Close School cricket 1st XI. **3** With wife Tuze. **4** With nephew John.

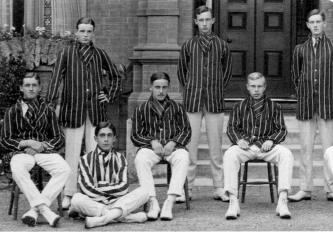

children
grandchildren
great-grandchildren
great-great-grandchildren
great-great-great-grandchildren

Major **Ronald William 'Ronnie' BRAKSPEAR**

b. Friday 12th November 1875 at home, in Henley-on-Thames, Oxfordshire, England
d. at about 3 p.m. on Saturday 2nd October 1915 in 20 General Hospital, Étaples, Pas-de-Calais, France
(after amputation of leg shattered in action during the first day of the Battle of Loos)
Time on Earth: 39 years, 10 months, 21 days — Buried, CWGC gravestone, 7 known memorials

1830 1840 1850 1860 1870 1880 1890 1900 1910 1920 1930 1940 1950 1960 1970 1980 1990 2000 2010

Practically born into a directorship of Brakspear's Brewery, he enjoyed a comfortable and privileged life only interrupted by service during the Boer War with the Royal Buckinghamshire Militia in Ireland. Two years to the day before the Battle of Loos, his wife of 10 years petitioned him for divorce on grounds of cruelty, adultery & desertion – and with no response from him, this was granted. After the outbreak of war, he sold a painting which proved to be an old Dutch Master for not much less than £1 million in today's money – part of these proceeds he put towards the conversion of Henley Town Hall into a hospital. He was an excellent shot and claimed the killing of a German sniper 11 days after arriving in France. His mother and brother arrived at his bedside just half an hour before he died of wounds received from a shell burst at Loos.

Stained glass window: His most illustrious forebear was Nicholas Breakspear (the spelling being how Ronald's name was said) who as Adrian IV was the only English Pope thus far, and who wore the symbol of a bee on his mitre. This same symbol was later adopted by Brakspear's Brewery who still use it today, though the family is no longer involved in the business. The feather is from his parrot.

—

1 As a young man. 2 Mother Florence. 3 On the ranges at Bisley.
4 Brother George.

1

2

3 ‹‹‹

4

Brakspear R. W.   Major R. Berks Regt.
Loos · · · · 1915

BRAKESPEAR : RONALD   BRAKSPEAR, R.

MAJOR R. W. BRAKSPEAR
ROYAL BERKSHIRE REGIMENT   R.W.BRAKSPEAR

R. W. BRAKSPEAR
R. W. BRAKSPEAR
MAJOR R. W. BRAKSPEAR

t, and I request that I may be appointed to a temporary
l of the war.

Ronald W. Brakspear.

Usual Signature of Candidate

B. D. Brigg.

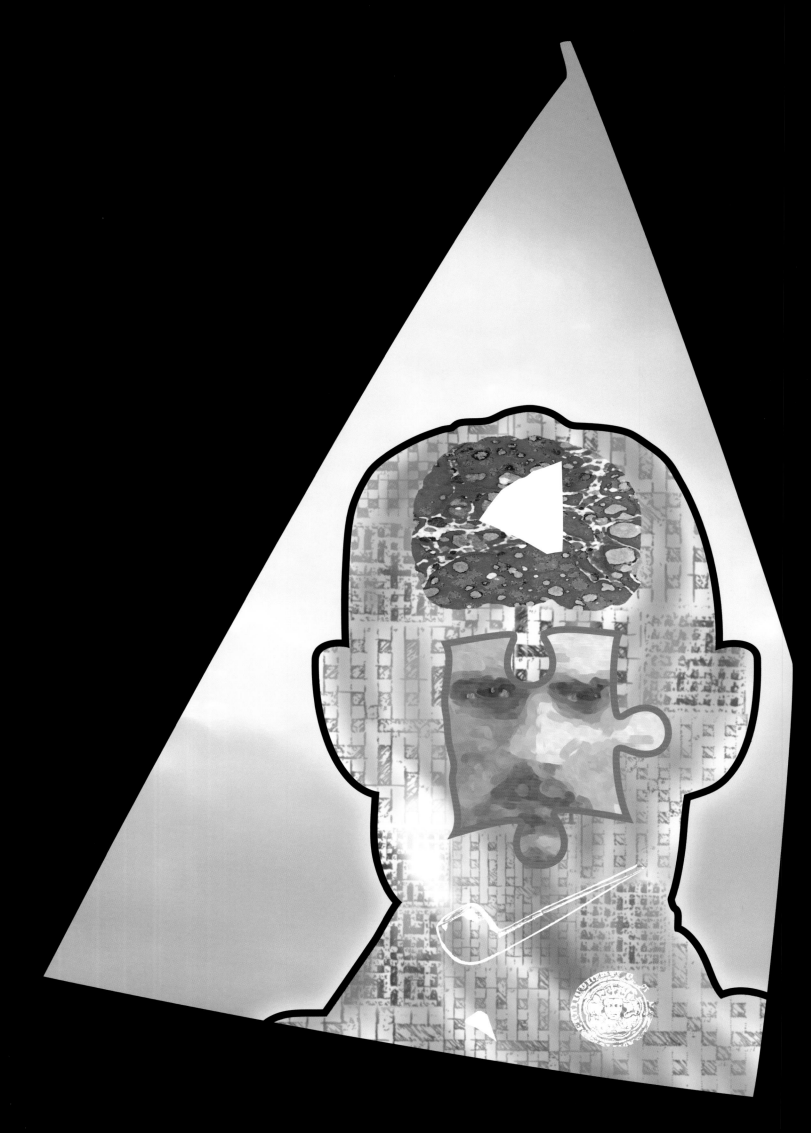

children
grandchildren
great-grandchildren
great-great-grandchildren
great-great-great-grandchildren

2nd Lieutenant **Brian Dudley BRIGG** later Captain in WW2

b. Wednesday 8th June 1892 in St Albans, Hertfordshire, England
d. Wednesday 24th December 1947 in Wembley, Middlesex, England (heart disease & kidney failure)
Time on Earth: 55 years, 6 months, 17 days
Cremated, ashes scattered, no known memorial

1830   1840   1850   1860   1870   1880   1890   1900   1910   1920   1930   1940   1950   1960   1970   1980   1990   2000   2010

Within 2 months of the group photograph being taken he had been transferred to the 26th Divisional Cyclist Company with whom he went to France (briefly), Salonika, Serbia, Bulgaria and Transcaucasia, ending the war as the quartermaster of a cyclist battalion. He had trained as a solicitor but spent his civilian career in a Continental import business which made use of his linguistic talents (he ritually said Goodnight to his daughter in 20 languages), and would complete the Daily Telegraph crossword in the 6-minute train journey to work. Suffered from rheumatism from very early on and shrank in height, that and his baldness he attributed to his wartime tin hat. Served throughout WW2 in transport and supply,

being bombed day and night whilst in Woolwich, and seeing very little of his children from the time they were in their early teens. His daughter's fondest memories of him were from their annual fortnight's sailing holidays on the Norfolk Broads.

Stained glass window: His grandfather traced his family tree back to George III, but his mother's family tree is a mystery.

—

1 At school. **2** In WW1 pre-commission. **3** With wife Freda.
4 In WW2. **5** With son John & daughter Joy.

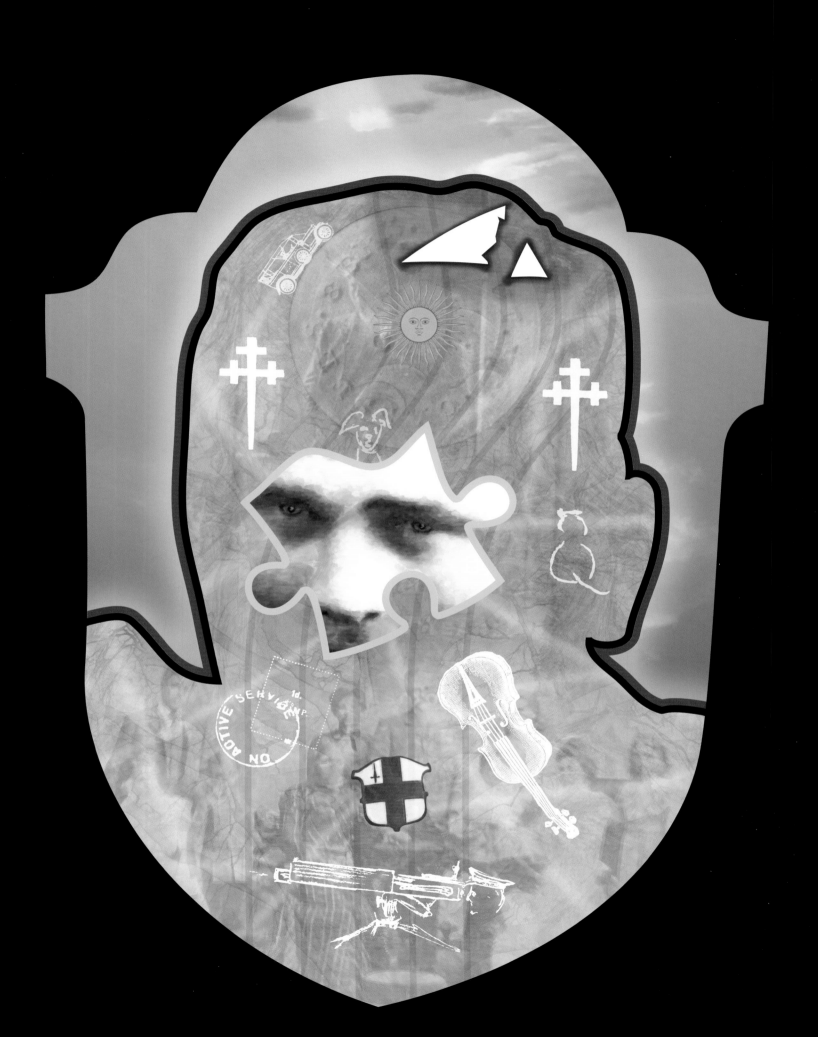

children
grandchildren
great-grandchildren
great-great-grandchildren
great-great-great-grandchildren

Lieutenant **Hugh Kennedy CASSELS** later Captain

b. Monday 12th February 1894 in Buenos Aires, Argentina
d. Saturday 25th September 1915, near Hulluch, Pas-de-Calais, France (killed in action on the first day of the Battle of Loos)
Time on Earth: 21 years, 7 months, 14 days
Buried, CWGC gravestone, 5 known memorials, also on the prefects board at his school

1830 1840 1850 1860 1870 1880 1890 1900 1910 1920 1930 1940 1950 1960 1970 1980 1990 2000 2010

The second youngest of 11 children, he was born and grew up in Buenos Aires before going to public school in England. A talented violinist and recent Mechanical Engineering graduate he was due to go to Toronto for a post-graduate course but felt that his OTC experience meant it was his duty to join up. Promoted quickly, he was a Captain and in charge of the Battalion's Machine Gun section at the age of only 21. His last letter concludes *"Today I blew a hole in a wall 18 inches thick with 50 rounds from a machine gun. Not bad work"*. Family letters show the struggle to deal with his death and within 3 months his father had died, heartbroken. A brother-in-law and a brother were also killed in action within a year.

Stained glass window: The cat & dog & machine-gun drawings are taken from the envelope of his last letter home.

—

1 The youngest in this picture (brother Alfred was still to come). Hugh is in his father Walter's arms at top right. Mother Elvina is just in front of Walter. His siblings are (back row) John, Dick (middle row) Bob, Ruby, Luza, & Frank standing at right (front row) Nellie, Gracie & Jessie.

1
—

The good life before the War: with his father &
surrounded by sisters; taking part in a steeplechase;
& in his digs at college.

GERMAN EMPLACEMENT

SPECIAL
POST

PASSED BY CENSOR
No 1996

FIELD

Miss E. L. Cassels.
10 Ornan Road
Belsize Park
Hampstead
London
England

Amongst Hugh's artefacts are his notes from
a machine-gun course and his letters
from France. These include his
drawings which show the boy-
ishness underneath the mature
exterior he needed to present for such a responsible
job. There is also one of
the most emotive items I
found during my work on
this project. It is small &
easily lost & easily missed,
but imagine receiving this
ID disc knowing that it
was taken from the body of
someone you loved deeply, and
seeing what looks like their blood
dried on the edge. These discs were
made of what is basically compressed
cardboard so it is no wonder that so many bodies could not be identified after the war when all
means of identification had disappeared or rotted
away.

Hugh's father Walter was in Buenos Aires when he received the news of his son's death. He wrote to his daughter Luza in England: "*The telegram from the War Office, abrupt and sudden as it was – hardly came as a shock – for when I heard of the terrible fighting in Flanders and understood that Hugh would be there leading his men, I knew what the risk was. I knew that our turn might be coming up at any moment to receive such news. And I also felt that he would be in the front ready to "lay down his life for his friends" and "greater love hath no man than this". But, oh – the pity of it, the pity of it all, as it seems to us. Quite independently of his being my boy, to see such a splendid, promising boy, such a magnificent fellow in every way, struck down in this way. It is hard indeed. But then I believe that he and all those other splendid young men who are fighting and falling are in a real sense becoming the saviours of the world, and their self sacrifice will contribute to the coming age of peace and goodwill and blessing. At present it is hard to take comfort from this, the loss to us is so real and so keen. It is only when we look further and higher that we can begin to understand this wonderful truth.*"

Hugh with father Walter, and youngest brother Alfred (right).

In amongst the letters of condolence Walter received was this one from Rev William Morris, which he then copied into a letter to his son Frank out in France:

Dear Mr Cassels
Please accept my assurance of comradeship of soul with you & all yours in the temporary loss you have sustained by the glorious promotion of your son Hugh Kennedy. To have voluntarily placed his splendid promising young manhood upon the altar of sacrifice in this stupendous crusade of world redemption, is glory indeed.
The new loneliness seems to call for heartfelt words of condolence and sympathy, but as I think of you, of all your family, and of the immortal pages of history on which his name is forever inscribed – not condolence but holy congratulations are what I would fain express. I know that all this passion and death is not unto death but unto life – that it is closely connected with the Cross of Calvary – that it is a continuation, and an extension of the ex-piational work of Christ, "a filling up of what is lacking in the sufferings of Christ" a part of God's process of eternal redemption, God's own warfare in Christ's name and nature against "Spiritual wickedness in high places". Thank God that your dear son is one of those heroes who counted not their life dear unto themselves, so that they might finish their course with joy – and who kept the great faith, and sealed it with his life.

This may be rather an extreme view but it is indicative of how from being a War that started for very material reasons, it came to be regarded by many as a crusade.

Hugh's brother Frank (on left with Hugh) wrote to his sisters in England:

Yesterday I went over and found Hugh's grave. It was rather difficult to find as he was not buried in the cemetery, but the description and direction was correct. Hugh's grave lies on the parapet of a captured German trench, it is amongst a few others, one of the advanced trenches in the line. It speaks for itself & tells us of a noble soul who died where he fell. I stopped only a short time. I tried to pray, but God knows my heart was too full. Still I came away greatly comforted. His grave has a small black cross at the head and then his name HK Cassels written in white ink. I shall some day get the chance and have it nicely fixed up.

Frank never got the chance. He was killed during the Battle of the Somme in 1916.

Also of
Captain HUGH KENNEDY CASSELS
8TH R. BERKS
FIFTH SON OF THE ABOVE
WHO WAS KILLED IN ACTION AT LOOS FRANCE
ON September 25th 1915.
AGED 21 YEARS.
Blessed of the Fa...

CAPTAIN
H. K. CASSELS
ROYAL BERKSHIRE REGIMENT
25TH SEPTEMBER 1915

HUGH KENNEDY CASSELS.
CAPT., ROYAL BERKS REGT.

H. K. CASSELS.

CASSELS, · HUGH · K.   H. K. Cassels

H. K. CASSELS   H. K. Cassels

children
grandchildren
great-grandchildren
great-great-grandchildren
great-great-great-grandchildren

2nd Lieutenant **Wilfrid Lawson CLARKE** later Lieutenant Colonel in WW2, MBE

b. Thursday 25 / 02 / 1886, Winkfield, Berkshire, England
d. Saturday 11 / 10 / 1975, Caversham, Reading, Berkshire, England (heart failure)
Time on earth: 89 years, 7 months, 17 days
Cremated, ashes buried in wife's grave, no known memorial

1830   1840   1850   1860   1870   1880   1890   1900   1910   1920   1930   1940   1950   1960   1970   1980   1990   2000   2010

His father and two elder brothers (all labourers) clubbed together to fund his education which meant that at the beginning of the war he was an assistant schoolmaster and was soon commissioned. Arriving in France post-Loos, he was buried unconscious by a shell in November 1915, rejoined to be wounded again on the Somme in July 1916, and thereafter was an instructor in a Physical & Bayonet Training School. Staying on with a regular commission in the Army Education Corps, his last education appointment was as headmaster of the Queen Victoria Military School in Dunblane, Scotland, before going on to be a staff officer in the UK in WW2. His only daughter never married and died intestate in 1999, and I helped the acting solicitor by finding the families of her fathers' brothers. One of her first cousins lived 3 miles from her and they had never met.

Stained glass window: The 2 stripes of decorative design work are taken from an embroidered silk scroll that was presented to him when he left his post as commandant of a military school in India in 1934, and which included the classic lines: *"Your frequent utterances such as 'Boys should be seen not heard,' 'Mind your business' will ever remain in our minds and be a source of inspiration to us in your absence".*
—

1 King George's Royal Indian Military School, Ajmer, in 1929. **2** With wife Ivy. **3** Daughter Margôt. **4** At Queen Victoria Military School, Dunblane.

1

2

3 ‹‹‹

4

children
grandchildren
great-grandchildren
great-great-grandchildren
great-great-great-grandchildren

65

Lieutenant **Cecil Stedman CLOAKE** later Captain, MC

b. Friday 2nd March 1894 in Chatham, Kent, England
d. Tuesday 9th September 1969, in Wimbledon, Surrey, England (burst major blood vessel in the abdomen)
Time on Earth: 75 years, 6 months, 8 days
Cremated, ashes scattered, 2 known memorials

1830 1840 1850 1860 1870 1880 1890 1900 1910 1920 1930 1940 1950 1960 1970 1980 1990 2000 2010

His abilities were spotted and he was sent on a Staff course before the Battalion embarked for France. Held in reserve for the first attack at Loos, he was soon selected to be Adjutant and held that position through attacks on the Somme (including going out in the open under shellfire to reorganise two companies who had lost their officers, winning an immediate field award of the Military Cross and suffering a small shrapnel wound in the head) and at Passchendaele. Eventually responded to a second appeal to go back and resume his medical studies (there was a shortage of doctors) and left the battalion in January 1918. Dedicated the rest of his life to medicine and to his family. Always held onto a guilt that he had survived when so many others had not. In WW2 he ran a First Aid Post based in the All England Tennis Club at Wimbledon, and attended many bombing incidents during the Blitz of 1940 as well as the V1 & V2 attacks late in the War. During their own military service, his son and grandson both wore his Sam Browne belt and sword with enormous pride.

Stained glass window: The outside frame shape is from the doorway of his surgery in Queen's Road, Wimbledon from where he practised for 36 years as a much-loved general practitioner. His Military Cross and campaign medals were stolen from his son's home in a burglary on 31st May 1985.

—

1 Parents Alfred & Elizabeth with Cecil's older siblings. 2 Cecil's wife-to-be Maude, wearing a Royal Berkshires' button that Cecil had had made into a brooch. She wrote to him every day when he was away during the War, and they were married in 1920.

1

2

»»
"So we went on learning to fight and kill with as much detachment as if we were learning a new skill."

During the Battle of the Somme: *"The Germans had recently been shelling the wood with gas shells. I was coughing badly and decided to put on my gas mask: knowing well the path, this should have been little handicap, but being very weary I must have stepped to one side and fell into a large shell hole three quarters full of filthy muddy water. I managed to scramble out. I need hardly say this did not enhance my feeling of well being, but it did disclose my vocabulary! "*

"Years later I often asked myself why I had joined the Army. I was not hot with patriotic feeling; I did not believe that Britain was in any real danger. I was not under any pressure from public opinion. I did not enlist in a herd rush of chums, I went alone.

I went at a signal from the unknown. There came out of the unclouded blue of that summer (1914) a challenge that was almost like the conscription of the spirit; little to do really with King and Country and flag waving. A challenge to what I felt was my untested manhood. It was the idea of not refusing a challenge; a test, like some tribes' initiation into manhood."

"I think it was in January 1917. It was my first day back off leave in England, when there walked into the Orderly room, in the middle of the morning, Major Douglas Tosetti. He had had an accident to his leg some days ago and had neglected the wound, which was now septic and discharging. The M.O. was on leave and, of course, every one knew that I had been a medical student. Being somewhat short tempered and trying to catch up on my accumulation of paper work, I said shortly, "It is the limit absolutely". This was my favourite expression when I was irritated. However, we got to work on the leg with hot bathing and hot compresses and in a few days the wound was clean and healing.

The next time Tosetti went on leave he brought back for me a silver pocket spirit flask, inscribed with my name, and engraved across it he had put "It is the limit absolutely"! I still have that flask."

"I sometimes wondered if I had a charmed life, and what I was being saved for!"

1 On left, with First Aid post at All England Tennis Club, Wimbledon, during WW2. **2** Maude & Cecil on right at son John's wedding, 1956. **3** With son & grandson, 1960. **4** Cecil, 1915. **5** Grandson John in the Royal Regiment of Fusiliers in the 1980s with his grandfather's sword.

DR. CECIL STEDMAN CLOAKE · M.C.
2 MARCH 1894 – 9 SEPTEMBER 1969

IN MEMORY OF DR. C. S. CLOAKE 1894-1969

LIEUT. C S CLOAKE

Cecil S. Cloake

In Loving Memory
of
HAROLD
2ᴺᴰ LIEUT 5ᵀᴴ ROYAL BERKSHIRE REGT
YOUNGEST SON OF
Mʳ AND Mʳˢ PERCY COHEN
OF READING
WHO DIED 18ᵀᴴ JULY 1915 5675.
AGED 19 YEARS
WE THINK OF HIM IN SILENCE
NO EYES CAN SEE US WEEP
YET EVER IN OUR ACHING HEARTS
HIS MEMORY SHALL WE KEEP
MAY his dear soul rest in Peace

Harold Cohen.

H. COHEN

children
grandchildren
great-grandchildren
great-great-grandchildren
great-great-great-grandchildren

2nd Lieutenant **Harold COHEN**

b. Saturday 25th April 1896 in Reading, Berkshire, England
d. at 2.55 p.m. on Sunday 18th July 1915 in Reading, Berkshire, England (pneumonia & blood poisoning caused by a strangulated hernia)
Time on Earth: 19 years, 2 months, 24 days
Buried, gravestone, 1 known memorial

Came back from working in his father's tobacco business in Antwerp to join up, adding a year to his age to ensure he was eligible to serve overseas. His army medical noted that he had a slight hernia at the scar from where his appendix has been removed, but with support from a belt it was considered he was not unfit for military service (!). 5 months later he fell ill whilst training – the hernia had become septic. His funeral attracted a large write-up in the local paper under the heading *"End to a Promising Career"* (showing the gulf between the view from the home front and the reality of what was going on in the trenches). After a long search complicated by name changes to hide from anti-Semitism, I found his nephew who was old and ill and professed to have never have heard of his uncle Harold.

Stained glass window: Harold's grave, including a Hebrew inscription, is in Golders Green Jewish Cemetery. I was probably the only person to have visited it in at least the last 50 years.

—

1 At Silver Wedding party for his parents Percy & Jessie in 1913
(Harold is 3rd from left in 2nd row from front, Percy 7th & Jessie 8th).

1

children
grandchildren
great-grandchildren
great-great-grandchildren
great-great-great-grandchildren

2nd Lieutenant **George Bertrand COOTE** later Lieutenant

b. Friday 22nd May 1896 in Brompton, Kensington, London, England
d. Monday 27th May 1918 in the area of Pontavert, Aisne, France (killed in action with 50th Battalion Machine Gun Corps on the first day of the German attack on the Chemin des Dames during their Spring Offensive)
Time on Earth: 22 years, 0 months, 6 days — Body never found, no known grave, 3 known memorials

1830   1840   1850   1860   1870   1880   1890   1900   1910   1920   1930   1940   1950   1960   1970   1980   1990   2000   2010

He was following his father into the law when war broke out. Left behind when the 8th Royal Berkshires embarked for France, he rejoined the battalion after Loos. Transferred to the Machine Gun Corps in early 1916 and suffered severe bruising when he was buried by a wall that collapsed after being hit by a shell in Ypres in 1917. Having lost 2 sons in the War*, his mother devoted herself for many years to creating needlework products which enabled a crippled ex-serviceman to earn his living by selling them in the street outside Harrods. The family died out in 1978, and a book containing detailed family trees with the coats of arms of his many illustrious forebears ended up in the safekeeping of his nephew's neighbour, from whom I passed it on to a distant cousin.

Stained glass window: He was in the Cricket 1st XI for Radley College, whose coat of arms is at top right, and whose War Memorial arch provided the shape for the outer frame.

* His elder brother Captain Richard Markham Coote was also in the 8th Royal Berkshires though was away at the time of the group photograph and was killed in the second attack at Loos.

—

1 Mother Sybil, smallest of 14 children in front of her parents.
2 Mother Sybil. 3 Father Charles. 4 Brother Richard. 5 Brothers Richard & Philip. 6 On right with Harold Woodford at Sandhill Camp.

1
2

3
4

5

6

GEORGE·BERTRAND·COOTE

LIEUTENANT COOTE G.B.

G·B·COOTE·
ROYAL WEST KENT REGT·

George B. Coote.

children
grandchildren
great-grandchildren
great-great-grandchildren
great-great-great-grandchildren

2nd Lieutenant **Alfred Percival 'Alf' DOBSON** later Major in WW2, MC

b. Wednesday 2nd October 1895 in Newcastle-upon-Tyne, Northumberland, England
d. Thursday 21st June 1984 in Darlington, Durham, England (burst ulcer)
Time on Earth: 88 years, 8 months, 20 days
Cremated, ashes scattered, no known memorial

1830 1840 1850 1860 1870 1880 1890 1900 1910 1920 1930 1940 1950 1960 1970 1980 1990 2000 2010

Having survived several major actions during WW1, he had to go through it all again in WW2. Between the wars he worked in the prison service and kept in shape by being a football referee (he was the linesman for two FA Cup finals) and was still able to fit into his First World War uniform when he was called up in 1939. During the Fall of France, he was sent to St Nazaire to board the liner Lancastria. Being fastidious (he wore two watches to ensure punctuality), he was with the ship's barber when the German bombs landed. His abilities as a champion swimmer enabled him to remain afloat in the oily water for 4 hours, including hoisting a man who couldn't swim any more onto a log. Over the next 5 years he served in Egypt, Eritrea, the Sudan and finished up in Italy just 40 miles from where he was at the end of WW1. Organising and taking part in Remembrance events for both wars was a constant thread through the rest of his long life.

Stained glass window: The Butlin's badge is from a holiday photograph in the 1950s – he was regularly on the camp organising committees.

---

1 At bottom left, in water polo team with son Vic at top right.
2 On right, with wife Beatrice, at Butlin's. **3** 2nd from right at unveiling of a picture of the Sinking of the Lancastria.

1

3

5

Captain **Lionel Huddlestone EDWARDS**

b. Monday 25th August 1884 in Stroud Green, near Finsbury Park, London, England
d. Thursday 13th January 1944 in Chelsea, London, England (heart failure)
Time on Earth: 59 years, 4 months, 20 days
Buried in family plot, no known memorial

1830   1840   1850   1860   1870   1880   1890   1900   1910   1920   1930   1940   1950   1960   1970   1980   1990   2000   2010

Missed the battalion's first attack at Loos due to trench fever, but recovered in time to lead a company into the second attack, being shot in the left groin with the bullet emerging from his left buttock (much to the amusement of Charles Bartlett). The wound became infected with gas gangrene and also led to sciatica but eventually he became fit enough to serve on the staff in Egypt, where he had bouts of influenza and sandfly fever. In later life he had to have both legs amputated and was remembered by his godson Larry (son of Gerald Robinson) as "Lionel the legless", who though delicate in body was a powerful man and steadfast friend of his father's.

Stained glass window: He is not named on the family grave where he is buried but there were marigolds and primulas growing nearby and I thought they were a way of showing the warmth with which he was remembered by his two godsons (he was also godfather to a son of Gordon Marsh) and also by my grandmother.

—

1 At Sandhill Camp, 1915. **2** The tree growing out of his family's grave, 2008.

1
—

2
—

CAPTAIN. L.H. EDWARDS

Lionel H. Edwards

Signature of Officer or Man.

ERIC FOOT

2nd Lieutenant, Royal Berkshire Regiment, Missing, October, 1915.

FOOT D. E. FOOT D. E. ERIC FOOT

D. E. Foot D.E.FOOT

children
grandchildren
great-grandchildren
great-great-grandchildren
great-great-great-grandchildren

2nd Lieutenant **Douglas Eric 'Eric' FOOT**

b. Sunday 6th December 1896 in Pulborough, Sussex, England
d. Wednesday 13th October 1915, near Hulluch, Pas-de-Calais, France (killed in action in the 8th Royal Berkshires' second attack during the Battle of Loos)
Time on Earth: 18 years, 10 months, 8 days
Body never found, no known grave, 5 known memorials

1830   1840   1850   1860   1870   1880   1890   1900   1910   1920   1930   1940   1950   1960   1970   1980   1990   2000   2010

Joining up almost straight from school, photographs show him fully engaged in the life of a junior officer, on his motorbike and doing first aid training. Rejoined the battalion in the first wave of reinforcements after the first day at Loos, and 8 days later was posted "wounded & missing". He hadn't lied about his age but at 18 he was a year younger than the minimum required for overseas service (a fact that was pointed out by his mother in a letter to the War Office). Eric's brother also died young – an air ace and friend of Albert Ball, he miraculously survived the War but was killed when his plane crashed in an air race in 1923. A painting of the young family from 1902 appears to be a premonition – in the foreground his mother and sister sit in the sunshine whilst Eric and his brother are shown disappearing up a path into the dark woods behind.

Stained glass window: The golden eagle is a helmet plate picked up on the battlefield of Waterloo by his grandfather's uncle. No doubt like all of these men he would have been inspired by tales of Waterloo from exactly a century before.

—

1 On rocking horse, with brother Leslie (also shown in inset). 2 *'Tea in the Garden'* painted by Ethel Walker (later a Dame) in the garden of the family home in Pulborough. Back: Eric & Leslie. Front: mother Maud & sister Enid (who lived until 1990).

1

2

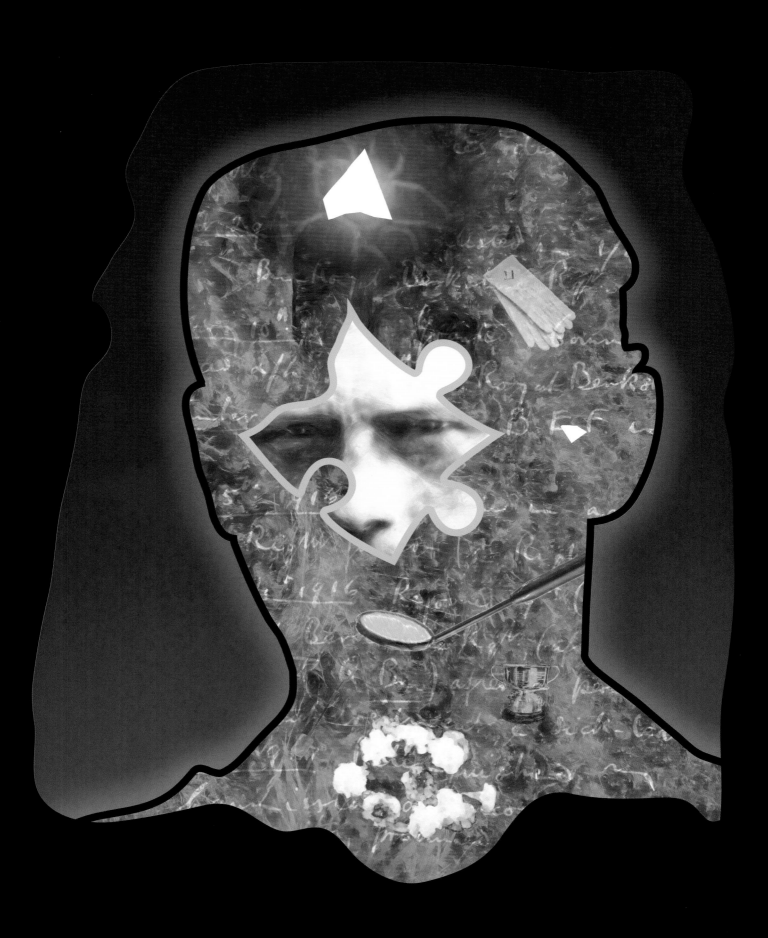

2nd Lieutenant Frederic Clifford 'Eric' GARDENNER later Lieutenant

b. Tuesday 4th July 1893 in Camborne, Cornwall, England
d. Tuesday 3rd May 1938 in Truro, Cornwall, England (cancer of the pancreas)
Time on Earth: 44 years, 10 months, 0 days
Buried and commemorated on family grave

1830　1840　1850　1860　1870　1880　1890　1900　1910　1920　1930　1940　1950　1960　1970　1980　1990　2000　2010

The son of an Art School headmaster, he left his dentistry studies in Reading to enlist in the local regiment. Rejoined the battalion to help reorganise after the second attack at Loos, and was hit by shrapnel in March 1916. Medical reports only mention a slight thigh wound and a compound fracture of his right arm (which went septic), but he ended up having to relinquish his commission through ill health, and his first cousin said that he had shrapnel in his brain that led to him having epileptic fits every few weeks. He did not let this stop him living life to the full as a busy and popular dentist who was greatly involved in the local community in commerce, in infant welfare, and as a musical and theatrical performer, and a Freemason. A huge number of people attended his funeral.

He, his parents & siblings share one grave, except for his brother Jack whose war grave in France bears the epitaph "Our Dear Boy".

Stained glass window: The cup is from the golf club he co-founded along with Thomas Lawrence in Cornwall – he is also named on three honours boards in the clubhouse.

---

1 Parents Frederick & Cecilia. 2/3 On left with brother & sister. 4 As a boy. 5 Sister Cicely lived to be 89. 6 Father Frederick with his sons Henry, Eric & Jack.

1930   F. C. GARDENNER   1932   F. C. GARDENNER

1932. F.C.GARDENNER.   1936 F C GARDENNER

FREDERIC J C GARDENNER 1893 1938

F. C. Gardenner.

(Usual signature of candi

Glen. David Corse. Lieut. Royal Berks Regt. ✠

LIEUT. D. C. GLEN D.C. Glen D. C. GLEN

D. C. GLEN GLEN · DAVID · C.

David C Glen Jun.?

(Usual signature of candidate)

children ——————
grandchildren ——————
great-grandchildren ——————
great-great-grandchildren ——————
great-great-great-grandchildren ——————

Lieutenant **David Corse GLEN**

b. at 1.30 a.m. on Wednesday 27th June 1894 in Greenock, Renfrewshire, Scotland
d. Saturday 25th September 1915, near Hulluch, Pas-de-Calais, France (killed in action on the first day of the Battle of Loos)
Time on Earth: 21 years, 2 months, 30 days
Buried, CWGC gravestone, 5 known memorials

| 1830 | 1840 | 1850 | 1860 | 1870 | 1880 | 1890 | 1900 | 1910 | 1920 | 1930 | 1940 | 1950 | 1960 | 1970 | 1980 | 1990 | 2000 | 2010 |

He and his father and his grandfather were all named David Corse Glen, all were born in Scotland, and all were mechanical engineers – his grandfather also being a renowned geologist who amassed a magnificent collection of minerals and fossils that forms the basis of the collection in the Kelvingrove Museum in Glasgow. Graduated from the same course as Hugh Cassels in London. Had an Army medical on 17th August 1914, then on 21st August set out to motorcycle up to Scotland with two friends, seemingly without a care in the world. He teamed up with Hugh Cassels in leading the Machine Gun Section. Survived by his sister who went on to have three long-lived daughters, each of whom has had children. Not much remains of him as a person, but his loss is remembered.

Stained glass window: 778 is the registration number of his headstone. The outside frame shape is from the war memorial at Watford Grammar School.

—

1 › 3 With mother Mary & sister Joan. **4** On left, with his sister's future husband Colin & Colin's elder brother in 1914. **5** Sister Joan in 1914.

1 › 3
___

4
___

5
___

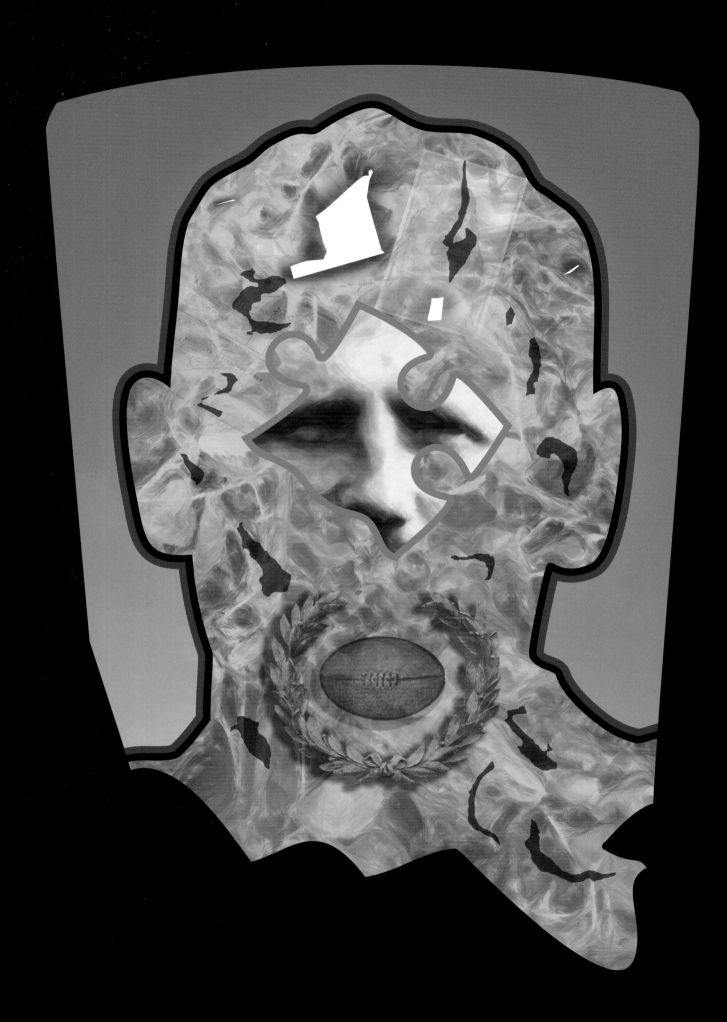

children
grandchildren
great-grandchildren
great-great-grandchildren
great-great-great-grandchildren

Captain Douglas Murray HANNA

b. Sunday 13th April 1873 in Honor Oak, Camberwell, Surrey, England
d. Saturday 25th September 1915, near Hulluch, Pas-de-Calais, France (killed in action on the first day of the Battle of Loos)
Time on Earth: 42 years, 5 months, 13 days
Buried, CWGC gravestone, 6 known memorials

1830 1840 1850 1860 1870 1880 1890 1900 1910 1920 1930 1940 1950 1960 1970 1980 1990 2000 2010

His parents must have been relieved he made it through childhood (3 of his 4 siblings died young), though in adulthood he can only have seen his family when on leave from being a tea & produce broker in Ceylon. On the outbreak of war, he helped raise the Colombo Town Guard before returning to the UK to join up. He might have failed his medical due to very poor eyesight in one eye but for the comment *"I wish to emphasize that he is otherwise particularly fit and well built"*. Though a very popular sportsman who had won innumerable running and sporting trophies, he was not a socialite, "in fact few ladies knew him except by sight & name". He was remembered in In Memoriam notices in The Times until 1929, but all his family could show me were a few pieces of paper and the photograph of the cross that originally marked his grave.

Stained glass window: The wreath comes from the civic war memorial in Penge, South London. Metal thieves stole one of the plaques from the memorial in 2011 and a photograph I had posted online was used to be able to make a replacement.

—

1 During battalion sports day, juggling? **2** Watching cricket, between William Walton & Douglas Tosetti. **3** His parent's grave in 2009.

1

2

3

DOUGLAS MURRAY HANNA

CAPT. D. M. HANNA
ROYAL BERKSHIRE REGIMENT

D. M. HANNA

D. M. HANNA

HANNA D. M.

HANNA. D. M.

CAPTAIN
D. M. HANNA
ROYAL BERKSHIRE REGIMENT
25TH SEPTEMBER 1915 AGE 43

Usual Signature of Candidate.

Geo. Henry Hewitt 1933   Revd. G. H. Hewitt 1933 – 1948   Revd. G. H. Hewitt
                                                            Vicar 1933-48

1927   George H.. Hewitt

IN MEMORY OF
GEORGE HENRY HEWITT. M.A.
FOR 15 YEARS
VICAR OF THIS PARISH
1933 – 1948

REV GH HEWITT M.A.   GEORGE HENRY HEWITT

Geo. Hy. Hewitt

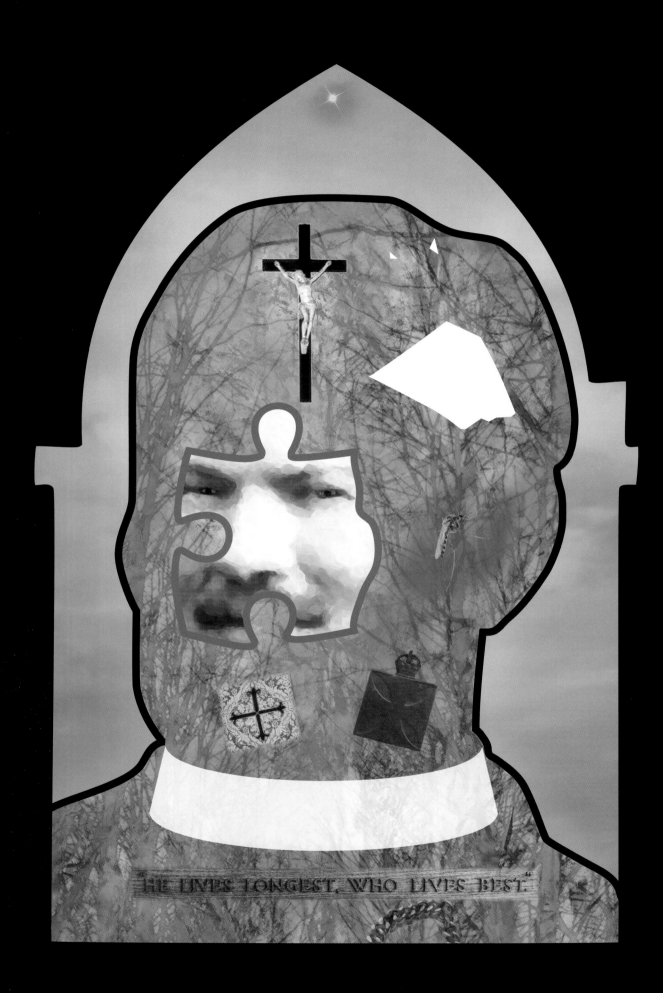

"HE LIVES LONGEST, WHO LIVES BEST."

children
grandchildren
great-grandchildren
great-great-grandchildren
great-great-great-grandchildren

Chaplain George Henry 'Henry' HEWITT

b. Wednesday 8th July 1868 in Liverpool, Lancashire, England
d. Tuesday 24th May 1949, Hitchin, Hertfordshire, England (stroke & heart disease)
Time on Earth: 80 years, 10 months, 17 days
Buried, gravestone, 1 known memorial, also listed on rolls of vicars in 2 churches

| 1830 | 1840 | 1850 | 1860 | 1870 | 1880 | 1890 | 1900 | 1910 | 1920 | 1930 | 1940 | 1950 | 1960 | 1970 | 1980 | 1990 | 2000 | 2010 |

He is an anomaly in the group photograph in that not only was he a chaplain, but he can only have joined the battalion a matter of days before the photograph was taken, and within weeks had been posted to be senior chaplain to the 26th Division (having been on the National Reserve pre-War). Caught malaria in Salonika, and also served in Egypt and France. Became a chaplain in the Territorials after the war. Endured a bleak few years as a vicar in the Fens, during which time his eldest son drowned in an accident in Canada. Was well-loved and looks at ease in his final parish in Hertfordshire. His remaining son was a chaplain to the Queen, but his grandchildren are "all pagans" though committed to public service.

Stained glass window: *"He Lives Longest, Who Lives Best"* is from the elaborately carved memorial to his son Jack.

—

1 With wife Ruth & daughter Theo. 2 With surviving son Gordon sitting next to him. 3 Son Jack. 4 In the 1930s. 5 With Army Cadet Force in the 1940s.

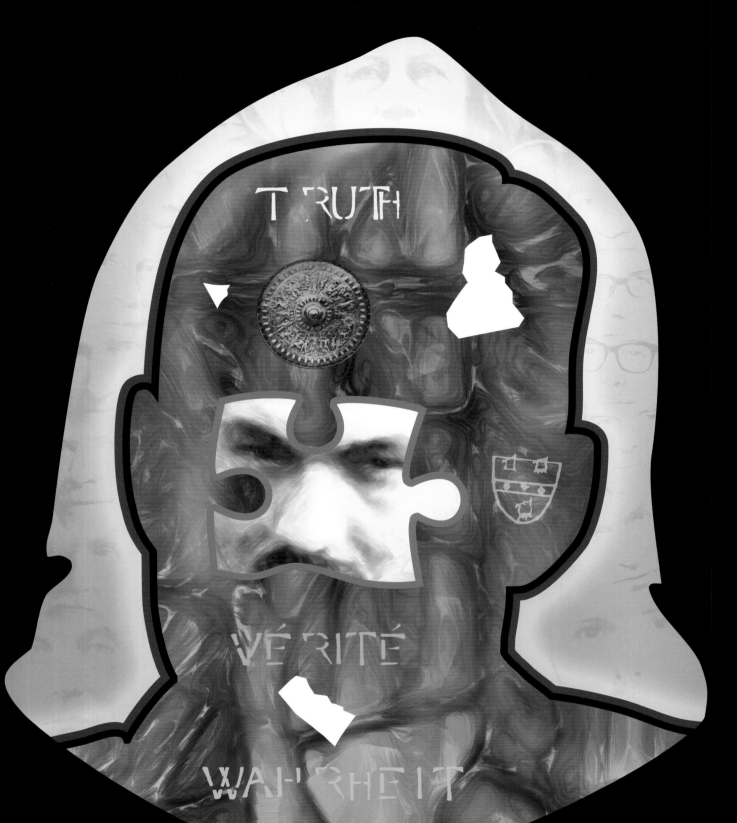

children
grandchildren
great-grandchildren
great-great-grandchildren
great-great-great-grandchildren

Lieutenant Basil Perrin HICKS

b. Saturday 22nd October 1892 in Sheffield, Yorkshire, England
d. Saturday 25th September 1915, near Hulluch, Pas-de-Calais, France (killed in action on the first day of the Battle of Loos)
Time on Earth: 22 years, 11 months, 4 days
Buried, CWGC gravestone, 6 known memorials

1830 1840 1850 1860 1870 1880 1890 1900 1910 1920 1930 1940 1950 1960 1970 1980 1990 2000 2010

At Rugby School, his housemaster was the father of the poet Rupert Brooke. He spent nine months in Germany before taking his degree in German and English, and on graduation in 1914 he went to Paris to learn French, soon returning home to join up at the outbreak of war. In the end though he is remembered more for his memorials than for the reality of who he was. His father was the first Vice Chancellor of the University of Sheffield and endowed a lecture series in his son's name that so far has seen 12 lectures given by big names such as Field Marshals Smuts, Alexander & Slim, and AJP Taylor, Roy Jenkins & David Owen. His uncle & aunt commissioned the renowned Pre-Raphaelite artist Henry Holiday to design the Great West Window, 4 metres high and 3 metres wide, in their parish church as a memorial to Basil and he appears as a helmeted Roman soldier in the bottom right hand corner.

Stained glass window: The Ashburton Shield is the Public Schools' shooting competition held annually at Bisley, and was won in 1909 by the team from Rugby School which included Basil and his brother Eric.

---

1 Father William. **2** Brother Eric. **3** Standing 2nd from right - brother Eric (seated 2nd from left) was team captain.

WINNERS OF ASHBURTON SHIELD 1909.

LIEUTENANT
BASIL PERRIN HICKS
ROYAL BERKSHIRE REGIMENT
25TH SEPTEMBER 1915 AGE 22

GREATER LOVE
HATH NO MAN THAN THIS
THAT A MAN LAY DOWN HIS LIFE
FOR HIS FRIENDS

B.P.HICKS   BASIL PERRIN HICKS

B.P.HICKS   BASIL·PERRIN·HICKS

BASIL·PERRIN·HICKS Lieut   BASIL·PERRIN·HICKS

Basil P. Hicks.   B.P.HICKS

LIEUT. WILLIAM GEORGE HOBBS
8TH ROYAL BERKSHIRE REGIMENT
W WHO FELL IN THE BATTLE OF LOOS
25TH SEPT. 1915, AGED 24
HE THAT LOSETH HIS LIFE FOR MY SAKE
SHALL FIND IT.

TO THE GLORY OF GOD AND IN MEMORY OF
LIEUTENANT WILLIAM GEORGE HOBBS
L.L.B. 8TH BATTALION ROYAL BERKSHIRE
REGIMENT WHO FELL IN ACTION AT HULLUCH
25TH SEPTEMBER 1915

W. G. HOBBS
W. G. HOBBS
HOBBS W. G.
HOBBS W. G.

William George Hobbs

WILLIAM GEORGE HOBBS
Lieut. 8th Royal Berks. Regt.

W. Geo Hobbs

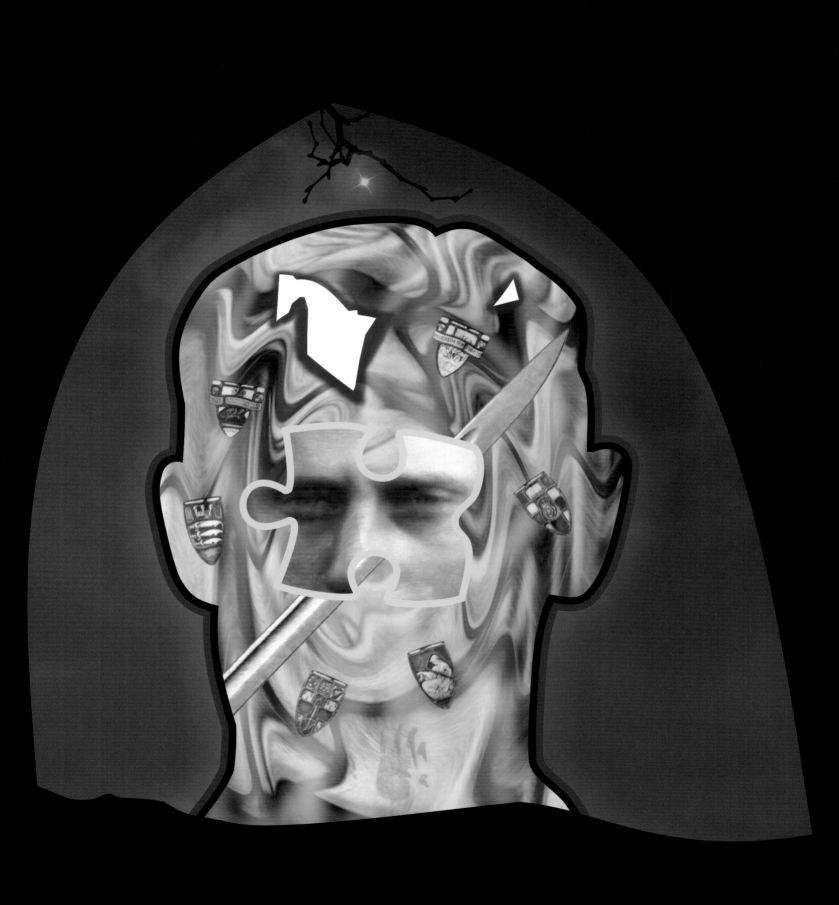

children
grandchildren
great-grandchildren
great-great-grandchildren
great-great-great-grandchildren

Lieutenant **William George 'Tod' HOBBS**

b. Tuesday 13th October 1891 in Hampstead, Middlesex, England
d. Saturday 25th September 1915, near Hulluch, Pas-de-Calais, France (killed in action on the first day of the Battle of Loos)
Time on Earth: 23 years, 11 months, 13 days
Buried on battlefield, not found after war, no known grave, 7 known memorials

His only sibling died married but childless aged 84, so it fell to the daughter of one of his first cousins to be my point of contact with his family. She was a self-professed "family history nut" and it was through her dedicated research that I found out in detail about the stained glass window that was commissioned by his parents and installed in their local Presbyterian church. It depicts him as St George in armour, and along the bottom are the coats of arms of his school, his university, the Law Society (he was a solicitor), Middlesex (for whom he played lacrosse), and the Royal Berkshire Regiment. By the time I got round to visiting, I found that the church had been sold for redevelopment as flats, and eventually I discovered that the window had been broken up and sold in two parts to Japan & Canada.

Stained glass window: The outside frame shape comes from his parents' grave which has an inscription to their son, and which I found lying flat and smashed into two pieces.

—

1 His parents' grave in the foreground.

1

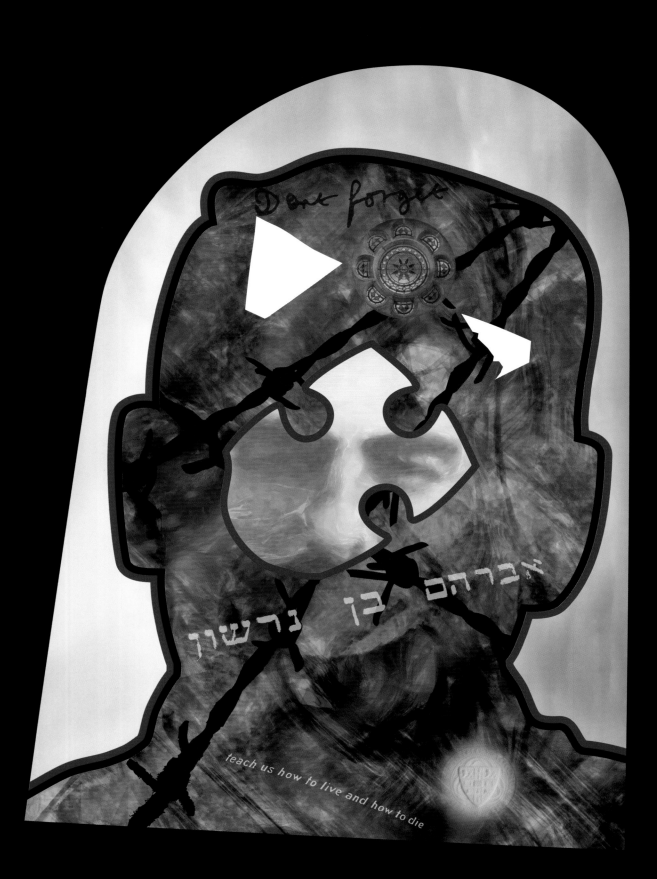

children
grandchildren
great-grandchildren
great-great-grandchildren
great-great-great-grandchildren

2nd Lieutenant **William Franklin George JOSEPH**

b. Saturday 30th December 1882 in Kensington, London, England
d. Monday 27th May 1918 near Berry-au-Bac, Aisne, France (killed in action with
2nd Royal Berkshires on the first day of the German attack on the Chemin des Dames during their Spring Offensive)
Time on Earth: 35 years, 4 months, 28 days — Body never found, no known grave, 8 known memorials

```
1830   1840   1850   1860   1870   1880   1890   1900   1910   1920   1930   1940   1950   1960   1970   1980   1990   2000   2010
```

From a cultured Jewish family who had their own family orchestra (his sister was an amanuensis to Gustav Holst and produced the manuscript for some of *The Planets)*. He followed his father in becoming a solicitor and also had poems published in newspapers before the War. Joined the battalion as a reinforcement out in France in October 1915, but suffered a complete nervous collapse during a bombardment on the Somme. It must have taken real courage to keep going after that, and nearly 2 years later he was killed trying to reorganise the companies of the 2nd Royal Berkshires that were in chaos under another bombardment. The family has no photographs of him (indeed they have no family albums from before WW1), and sadly all they have of him are some rather pompous letters written in his youth to his younger brother, and a hip flask that has recently been re-discovered.

Stained glass window: The phrase *"teach us how to live and how to die"* comes from the poem he wrote in remembrance of his father who died in October 1917. It appears on his father's grave, closely followed by the commemoration of his own death 7 months later.

—

1 Seated second from right, on the Somme, 1916.

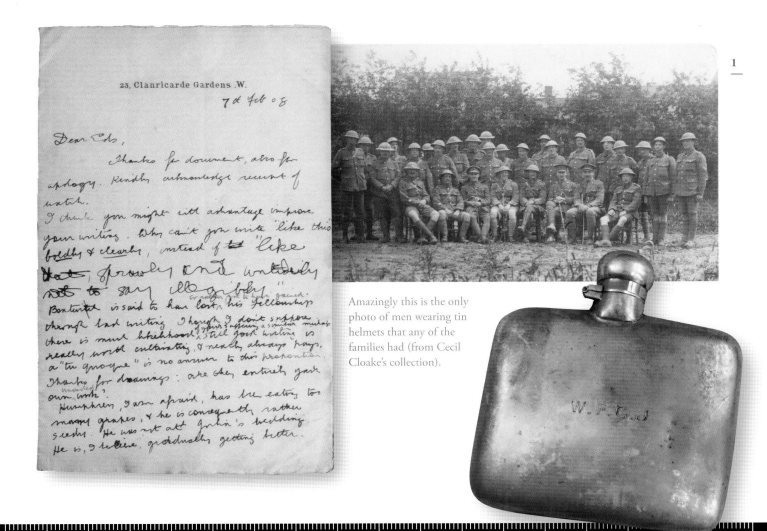

23, Clanricarde Gardens .W.

7 Feb 08

Dear Cds,

[handwritten letter]

Amazingly this is the only photo of men wearing tin helmets that any of the families had (from Cecil Cloake's collection).

W. F. G. J

WILLIAM FRANKLIN GEORGE JOSEPH 2ND ROYAL BERKSHIRE REGT 2ND LIEUT

SEC. LIEUT. WILLIAM F. G. JOSEPH, M.A.

When Death had set thy noble spirit free,
H took thine earthly form, but left us thee.
An influence immortal ever nigh.
To teach us how to live and how to die.

WRITTEN IN MEMORY OF HIS FATHER
BY
WILLIAM FRANKLIN GEORGE JOSEPH.
אברהם בן נרשון
2ND LIEUT. ROYAL BERKSHIRE REGIMENT.
BORN DEC 30TH 1882.
KILLED IN ACTION
NEAR BERRY AU BAC. FRANCE.
ON MAY 28TH 1918.
AGED 35.
THE PLACE OF HIS BURIAL IS UNKNOWN.

William F. G. Joseph

W. F. G. JOSEPH
2ND LT. BERKS. R

W. F. G. JOSEPH

WILLIAM FRANKLIN GEORGE JOSEPH

JOSEPH W. F. G.

Usual signature of ca

H. KEABLE   HAROLD C. L. KEABLE   2ND LIEUT

H.C.L.KEABLE   KEABLE. H.C.L.

To the glory of God, and in loving memory of Harold Charles Linford Keable, 2nd Lieut. 8th Service Battalion Royal Berkshire Regiment, younger and dearly loved son of Charles Henry Keable, Vicar of this Parish, and Constance Mary his wife, who gave his life at the battle of Loos, Sept. 25th 1915, aged 26. This Chapel is given by his Parents and Brother.

Usual Signature of Candidate

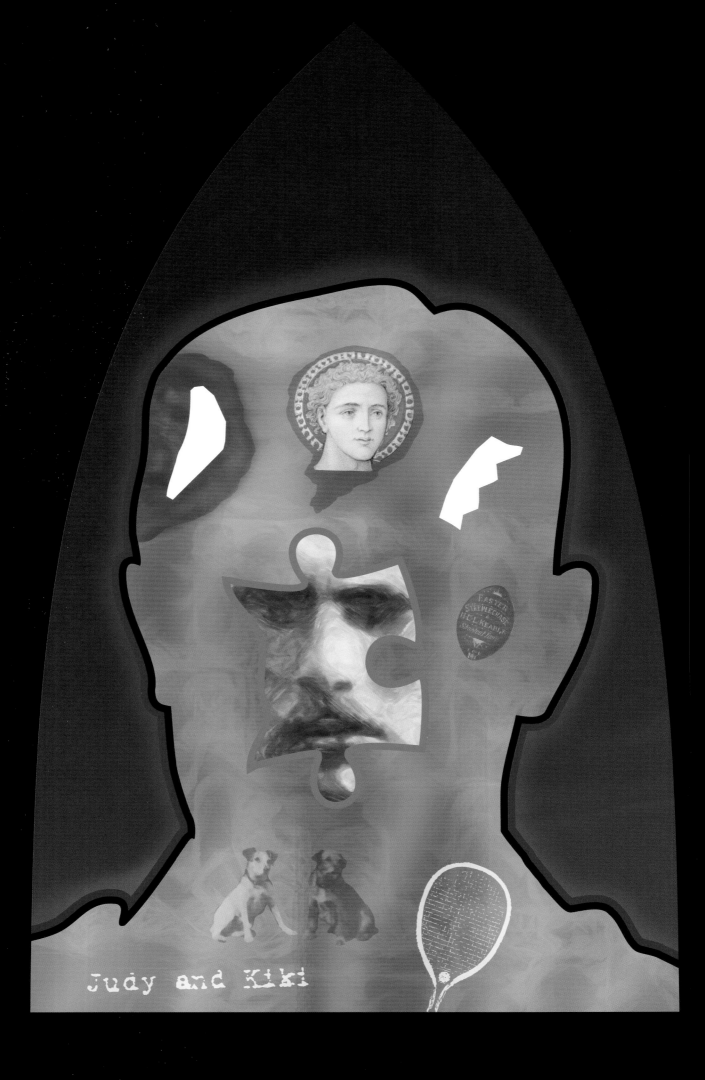

children
grandchildren
great-grandchildren
great-great-grandchildren
great-great-great-grandchildren

2nd Lieutenant Harold Charles Linford KEABLE

b. Friday 11th January 1889 in Luton Hoo, Bedfordshire, England
d. Saturday 25th September 1915, near Hulluch, Pas-de-Calais, France (killed in action on the first day of the Battle of Loos)
Time on Earth: 26 years, 8 months, 15 days
Buried, CWGC gravestone, 4 known memorials

1830　1840　1850　1860　1870　1880　1890　1900　1910　1920　1930　1940　1950　1960　1970　1980　1990　2000　2010

It is astonishing the change that can be seen between the wide-eyed youth of his school and Agricultural College photos and the square-jawed heavy-browed fellow when he's in the Army. Maybe it was the squinting in the Egyptian sun whilst working for the Aboukir Bay Company or had he developed a tougher exterior away from his sheltered upbringing? His loss was keenly felt and a chapel and a stained glass window are dedicated to him in the church where his father was the vicar for 33 years. His niece was the only remaining descendant of his parents, and since she died his medals have ended up in the hands of collectors.

Stained glass window: His will left his dogs Judy & Kiki to his father. Kiki, on the right, was still alive at the time of his brother's wedding in 1919.

—

1 Father Charles. **2** Mother Constance. **3** With elder brother Rupert.
4 The beginning of his will.

1

2 ⸾⸾⸾

3

4

W I L L In the event of my death I make the following bequests. To my dear Father, Charles Henry Keable, Priests, I give my Camera and all appliances belonging thereto, my tennis racquet and press, my two dogs Judy and Kiki, my travelling rug, two albums of photos taken by me, half the number of my pipes, my green suit case. To my dear Mother, Constance Mary Keable, I give the whole of my money, including Shares in the Capital & Counties Bank, The London & Brazillian Bank & the Orchestrelle Coy, my silver rose bowl & plinth. To my dear Brother, Rubert Henry Keable, I give all my books, my stamp collection, half the number of my pipes, my brown leather suit case. To my Dearest pal, Violet Catherine Bradney Pershouse,

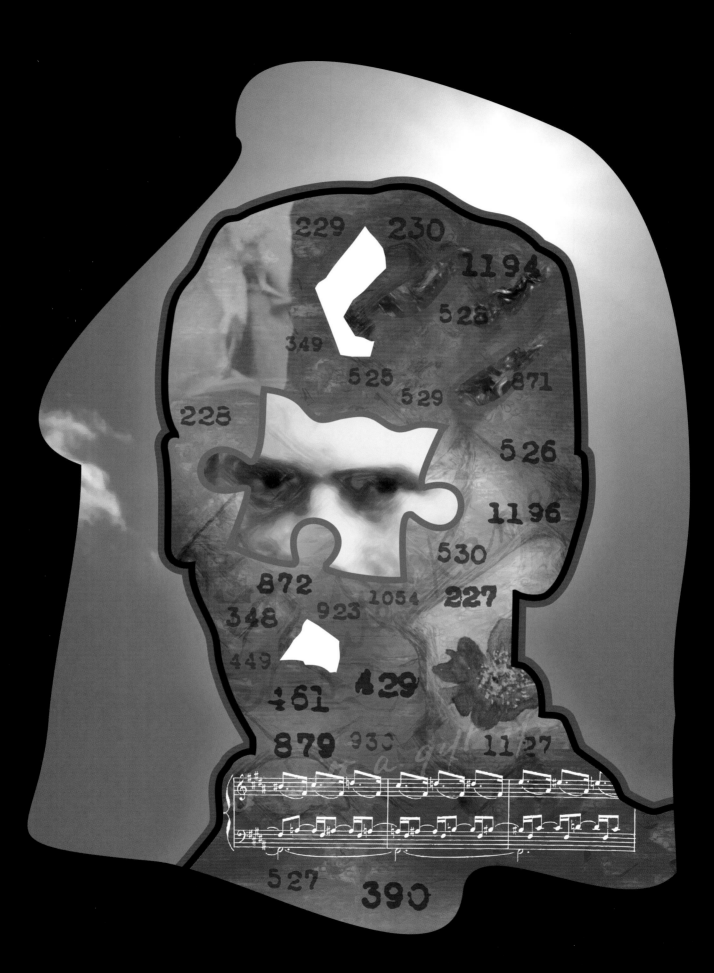

children ——————
grandchildren ——————
great-grandchildren ——————
great-great-grandchildren ——————
great-great-great-grandchildren ——————

2nd Lieutenant **Louis Arthur KLEMANTASKI**

b. Wednesday 12th August 1891 in Hackney, Middlesex, England
d. Saturday 27th May 1916 near Cité Calonne (now in Liévin), Pas-de-Calais, France
(killed in action by a German raiding party whilst out in no-man's land with a wiring party at night)
Time on Earth: 24 years, 9 months, 16 days — Buried, CWGC gravestone, 4 known memorials

1830   1840   1850   1860   1870   1880   1890   1900   1910   1920   1930   1940   1950   1960   1970   1980   1990   2000   2010

The son of Jewish emigrants from Poland via Holland, a friend described him as being "a very gentle gentleman; quite unfitted in every way to be a soldier". He had founded a quarterly journal of music criticism at the age of 18, and lived by the principles of Spiritual Idealism. His habit of regularly accompanying working parties into No-Man's Land at night swathed theatrically in his cape and completely unarmed led to his undoing – his body was found with 3 bayonet wounds. My contact with his family led to me attending their first full reunion in 20 years. His two nephews and niece were the only children of his four siblings, and as their father died very young, they knew next to nothing about Louis.

Stained glass window: The numbers are listed in his will and relate to his book catalogue, denoting gifts of specific volumes to his mother and a friend. The flower painting is from his poetry notebook which, with the permission of his wife, was kept as a memento of him by Cecil Cloake, his great friend and the man who had gone out into No-Man's-Land to recover his body.

—

1 Father Sidney, a horse-hair merchant. 2 Mother Lizzie - when her application for British citizenship in 1921 was being held up by foot-dragging bureaucracy she felt forced to point out that 3 of her sons had served in the War with her eldest Louis killed in action and mentioned "for gallant services in the field" in Sir Douglas Haig's dispatch of November 1916. Her youngest son Godfrey was in the Merchant Navy and changed his name to avoid anti-Semitism. As a consequence, none of Sidney & Lizzie's descendants bear the Klemantaski name. 3 Brother Godfrey. 4 Sister Alida - she went on to marry the poet Harold Monro, running the Poetry Bookshop in Bloomsbury, a centre for poets including Wilfred Owen & Robert Frost. She later became a renowned poodle breeder and international dog show judge. 5 Brother Benjamin.

1 › 3

4

5

To six brother Officers

All, all are gone, the old familiar faces
And those I loved the best are passed away
Not garnered by slow time, but in a day
Of hideous carnage, reft from friends and places
Dear, by lust of blood insatiably mean.
Dear P__ shall I forget your smile
Your glinting eyes, your noble Art and Style.
Nor you, large hearted H__ of prowess keen
In field and trench; S__ with whom a year
I gladly shared a room; W__ with whom
I've bathed and walked; you brilliant S__ the bloom
Of Greece; and sunny B__ devoid of fear.
All these are gone who, for the world, have done
Not less become rich fruit destroyed by Hun.

To A Sentinel — Obit 21.2.1916

I saw you as the first pale streaks of morn
Suffused the sky with faintest rose and green,
A sentry at your loophole stand, serene.
In that large trust that is of duty born.
I passed you by, still echoing in my ear
Your cheerful morning greeting "All is well".
A bullet pinged: without a word you fell,
Helmet and brain both pierced.
.......and now your bier
That same firestep under the dread loophole;
Beneath the tarpaulin I see your face
Livid and drawn, while all around the place
Is splashed with blood......
The sun sinks, the toll of tyranny is borne away.
But not the memory:
A noble offering's not forgot.

Louis Klemantaski re-joined the battalion out in France on the day of their disastrous second attack at Loos. The battalion he had known in training was practically gone and he could see the hideous aftermath. He wrote this poem and it was published in the *Reading Mercury* in March 1916. The likely missing names are Paramore, Hobbs (with whom Louis had been at school), Salman, Woodford, Spartali & Berlein.

The only soldier of the 8th Royal Berkshires to die on 21st February 1916 was Private John McDermott, aged just 19. 3 months later Louis Klemantaski met his own death, and the last line of this poem formed the epitaph on his headstone in Bully-Grenay Communal Cemetery.

Left to right: unknown Chaplain, Clifford Salman, Tod Hobbs, Louis Klemantaski, Wilfrid Clarke (the only survivor of those named, and in whose belongings this picture was found).

"A NOBLE OFF'RING'S UNFORGOT"

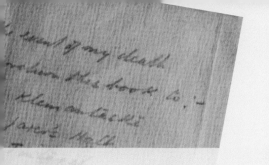

Trelegoe
Rock
Wadebridge

June 1st 1916

Dear Captain Cloake

Your letter was the first intimation I had of my terrible loss. I thank you from the depths of my heart for what you have done. Is it too much to ask you to let me know all details? Don't try to spare me. Have they marked the place where he lies so that if ever there is a time that I can get there I shall know?
He would have wished you to have what you would like of his, so please let me know if there is anything special.
To know him was to love him, & the proof of this in your letter touches me deeply. My loss is so incomprehensibly great that I cannot grasp it. It is only in the lonely days before me that I shall understand its full meaning.
I am deeply grateful to you & all the officers of the regiment for your sympathy.

I should like to see you if ever an opportunity occurs.

Yours very sincerely
Phyllis Klemantaski

1 His wife Phyllis. She sent a semi-hunter watch to Corporal Percy Holmes, who had stayed with her husband, killed a large Prussian Guard, and was involved in recovering her husband's body. Within a year she too had died - of tuberculosis. **2** Family reunion in 2001, with nephew Godfrey, niece Betty & nephew Louis in the front.

KLEMANTASKI, L. S. HAMPSTEAD

KLEMANTASKI, L. A.

LOUIS ARTHUR

LOUIS A. KLEMANTASKI

KLEMANTASKI

Louis Arthur Klemantaski sig.

T.B.LAWRENCE

2nd Lieutenant **Thomas Bernard 'Lawrie' LAWRENCE** later Lieutenant Colonel in WW2, MC

b. Wednesday 2nd January 1895 in Mandalay, Burma
d. Tuesday 4th December 1956 in Perranporth, Cornwall, England (kidney cancer)
Time on Earth: 61 years, 11 months, 3 days
Buried, no gravestone, no known memorial

children ——
grandchildren ——
great-grandchildren ——
great-great-grandchildren ——
great-great-great-grandchildren ——

1830 1840 1850 1860 1870 1880 1890 1900 1910 1920 1930 1940 1950 1960 1970 1980 1990 2000 2010

At the end of the first day at Loos, he was the only officer left fit and in contact with main body of the battalion and took over command at the age of only 20, winning the Military Cross. Seems to have inherited the luck of the Irish from his parents, because not only did he survive Loos, the Somme and Passchendaele and many scrapes in between, but he was posted to join the Indian Army on the very day that the Germans opened their Spring Offensive in 1918 when so many of his comrades were killed. He worked as a gold mining engineer in India & West Africa before rejoining the Indian Army in WW2 – serving as an internment camp commandant, then on a mission to Iraq & Syria, and ending up a controller of rice procurement in India. Returned to mining before retirement to Cornwall where his luck finally ran out. Nearly all of the 18 descendants of

his 2 children are planning to come to the exhibition.

Stained glass window: He had a tattoo of a heart on the front of his left forearm, acquired in his teens – both in keeping with his father (who was rather a Jack-the-lad who had been commissioned from the ranks in the Indian Army) and as a rebellion against his mother (who beat religion into him and left her husband to join a nunnery).

—

1 Parents John & Ellen. **2** Wedding in Rangoon, 1923. **3** Internment camp commandant, 1940. **4** With son Peter, wife Phyllis & daughter Moyra. **5** With wife & daughter on return from India, 1947.

The officers of the 8th Royal Berkshires (& other units) appear to have scratched their signatures into the inside of this cigarette case on the occasion of his leaving to take up his commission in the Indian Army just before the opening of the German Spring Offensive on 21st March 1918. Below is a listing of the officers of the battalion at that time along with their fates, yet another reminder of scale and suddenness of the destruction that could happen at any time on the Western Front:

Douglas Tosetti *killed 21st March 1918*

FD Phillips *transport officer, survived*

F Swaffield *joined 8RBR on 29th April 1917, fate unknown*

AA Turner *no record of his fate*

C Bland *captured 21st March 1918, killed 1919 in Russia*

GR Goodship *captured 21st March 1918*

CHC Byrne *captured 21st March 1918, battalion medical officer – hence 'Doc' below his name*

JC Gordon *killed 21st March 1918*

RW Crampin *joined 8RBR on 25th March 1917, wounded 31st March 1918*

N Williams *killed 21st March 1918*

C Gentry-Birch *captured 21st March 1918*

SAG Harvey *killed 21st March 1918*

EG King *killed 21st March 1918*

FM Sumpster *killed 21st March 1918*

RE Dewing *killed 4th April 1918*

H le G Sarchet *killed 4th April 1918*

N Langston *captured 21st March 1918*

EJ Mecey *captured 21st March 1918*

WCA Hanney *captured 21st March 1918*

DJ Footman *captured 21st March 1918*

TH Baker *wounded 21st March 1918*

HBF Kenney *wounded 25th March 1918*

JW Randall *wounded 24th March 1918*

HR Fenner *wounded & captured 21st March 1918*

G Capes *captured 21st March 1918*

WV Heale *captured 21st March 1918*

EF Johnson *captured 21st March 1918*

JR McMullen *captured 21st March 1918*

TH Roberts *missing 21st March 1918*

AG Williams *missing 21st March 1918*

JM Richardson *wounded 4th April 1918*

AW Morland *wounded 4th April 1918*

E Wallis *wounded 4th April 1918*

I wonder if he used this cigarette case in later life or would it have been too much to be reminded of those terrible times every time he had a smoke?

—

On the left are the widow of Thomas Lawrence's son Peter along with her 6 children, their spouses and 9 of her grandchildren - that's 15 people in this picture who owe their existence to Thomas Lawrence's exceptional luck. Thank you to Thomas' grandson Peter for deciphering the signatures and marking them up, and to Matilda at bottom right for pressing the self-timer button on the camera.

J C Gordon (Bang) — Norman Langston — ??James Clive?? — C F Amm BR

S Monhagan — G Fenwick

JENKS
CHERIOH
7-5-23

R J Masterton 1st TMB

Douglas Tosetti — C H C Byrne — Doc

H G Mackey

W V Heale — E Wallis

F D Phillips

A Rowden??

??J W Randall

E J Mecey

J H Weedon — C Gentry-Birch — W Hanney

G R Goodship

F Swaffield 10.6.16

R W Crampin

R E Dewing

F Moor

C Bland

A Gordon

A A Turner

R G Evans (SWB)

Tontolini

AMB

? Lawrance

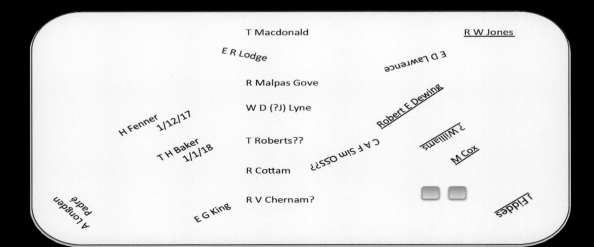

T Macdonald

R W Jones

E R Lodge

E D Lawrence

R Malpas Gove

W D (?J) Lyne

Robert E Dewing

H Fenner 1/12/17

T H Baker 1/1/18

T Roberts??

C A F Sim OSS??

J Williams

R Cottam

M Cox

A Longden padré

R V Chernam?

E G King

J Fiddes

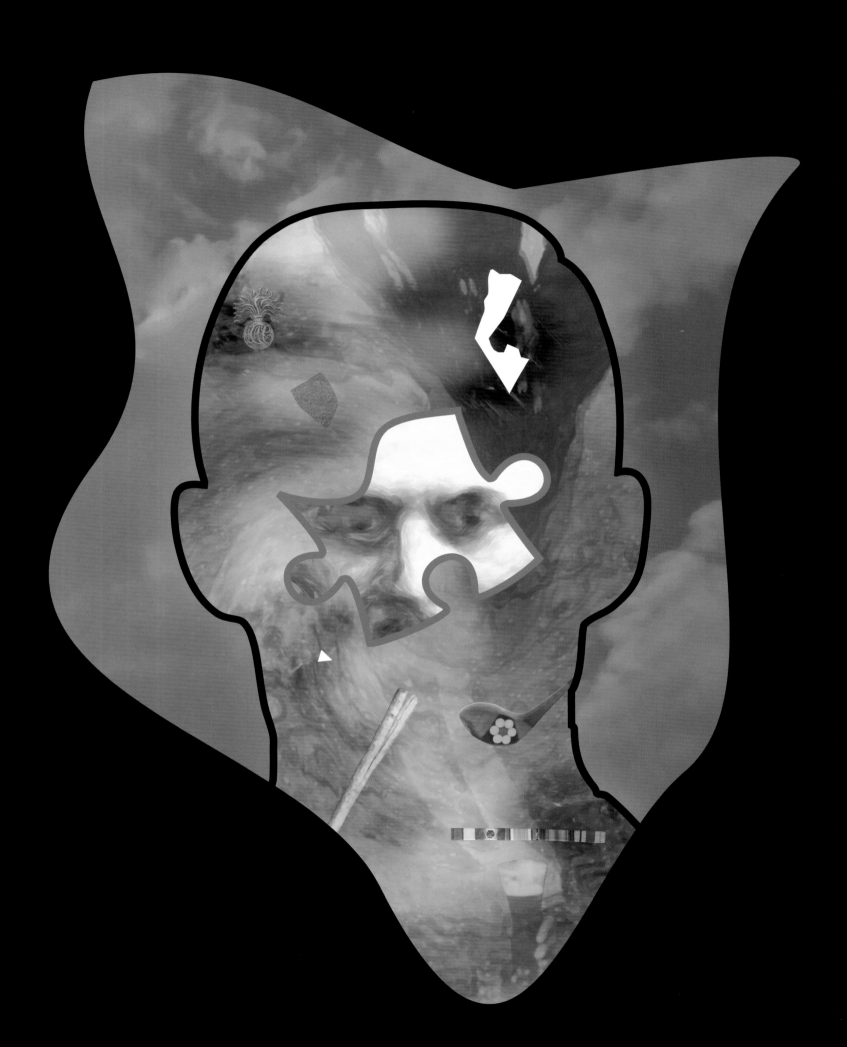

children 🏻🏻
grandchildren 🏻🏻🏻🏻🏻
great-grandchildren 🏻🏻🏻🏻🏻🏻
great-great-grandchildren
great-great-great-grandchildren

2nd Lieutenant **Gordon Fraser MARSH** later Captain & Quartermaster in WW2, MC

b. Sunday 26th March 1893 in Hampstead, Middlesex, England
d. Monday 9th January 1961 in Nakuru, Kenya (cause of death unknown)
Time on Earth: 67 years, 9 months, 15 days
Buried, gravestone

1830   1840   1850   1860   1870   1880   1890   1900   1910   1920   1930   1940   1950   1960   1970   1980   1990   2000   2010

The first of these men to get out to France and the only one to qualify for the 1914 Star campaign medal, he was shot in the head whilst serving with the Honourable Artillery Company as a private. On recovery, he was commissioned, only to be wounded in the shoulder on the first day at Loos. Arrived back out on the Somme in July 1916, and 12 days later won the Military Cross for leading a night raid. Gassed at High Wood in September, he was initially sent to India to convalesce before going to Kenya because the air was supposed to be better for his lungs – and that is where he eventually settled and served as an officer running POW camps in WW2. One son was wounded at Monte Cassino in 1944 and the other was Ernest Hemingway's pilot when he crashed (twice) in Africa, and later founded Air Seychelles.

Stained glass window: The cleft stick was mentioned by his son as being a standard way of transporting messages in Kenya – the piece of paper would be wedged into the cleft and handed to a runner to deliver.

—

1 A slice of Lone Tree - a famous landmark on the Loos battlefield - and now a paperweight. **2** With wife Christine and son Nigel.
3 With son Roy, the pilot.

1
—

2
—

3
—

G. F. Marsh.

IN LOVING MEMORY
GORDON FRASER MARSH M.C.
CALLED TO REST 9TH JAN 1961
UNTIL THE DAWN

G.F.MARSH

W. S. D. Oldman Capt. R. Berks. R

W. S. D. OLDMAN

W. S. D. OLDMAN

the war.

CAPTAIN
W. S. D. OLDMAN
ROYAL BERKSHIRE REGIMENT
25TH SEPTEMBER 1915 AGE 36

children
grandchildren
great-grandchildren
great-great-grandchildren
great-great-great-grandchildren

Captain **Wilfred Southey Deare OLDMAN**

b. Tuesday 11th March 1879 in Surbiton, Surrey, England
d. Saturday 25th September 1915, near Hulluch, Pas-de-Calais, France (killed in action on the first day of the Battle of Loos)
Time on Earth: 36 years, 6 months, 15 days
Buried, CWGC gravestone, 3 known memorials

1830 1840 1850 1860 1870 1880 1890 1900 1910 1920 1930 1940 1950 1960 1970 1980 1990 2000 2010

He was a tea planter in Ceylon before seeking action in the Boer War, ending up as a sergeant in the South African Constabulary. His tree is notable for the number of people who died before their time. He was an orphan at the age of 8, his mother dying in childbirth, and his father drowning in a freak shipping accident involving the Seine Bore. One elder brother disappeared overboard from a ship in the middle of the Arabian Sea, his sister lost 4 of her 6 children young (including one shot down in a bombing raid over Berlin in WW2) and a great nephew was shot dead by terrorists in Malaya. One great nephew I contacted had never heard of him and whilst a great niece has his Boer War medals, no-one in the family had a photograph of him.

Stained glass window: The Oldman coat of arms is a hand painted version belonging to his great niece.

—

1 Mother Helen. 2 Brother Richard (later Maj-Gen, CB, CMG, DSO). 3 In March 1915. 4 Training with 8th Royal Berkshires (including Cecil Cloake & Leslie Berlein).

children
grandchildren
great-grandchildren
great-great-grandchildren
great-great-great-grandchildren

Captain **Charles Gordon 'Gordon' PARAMORE**

b. Wednesday 1st April 1885 in St Pancras, London, England
d. Saturday 25th September 1915, near Hulluch, Pas-de-Calais, France (killed in action on the first day of the Battle of Loos)
Time on Earth: 30 years, 5 months, 25 days
Buried, CWGC gravestone, 8 known memorials

1830 1840 1850 1860 1870 1880 1890 1900 1910 1920 1930 1940 1950 1960 1970 1980 1990 2000 2010

The son of a doctor who was a grandee of the temperance movement, he showed a hint of rebellion, launching one of his father's cats off the roof with a parachute, and becoming an artist (his 3 surviving brothers all became doctors). Joined up from his studies at the Royal Academy, but seemingly out of duty rather than any great willingness (writing to his tutor to tell of his commission: *"I'm looking forward to the great time when this damned war will be over"*). Became a great chum of Leslie Berlein ("thick as thieves") – on the eve of Loos, they both removed the stars from their cuffs so as not to stand out like officers but were told to replace them. After Loos, his sister Edith asked the War Office where to apply for information "as the regiment seems to have been pretty well wiped out". Only one of his paintings is known still to exist. It is of trees.

Stained glass window: The star motif at the bottom is the crest on a piece of family silver shown to me by his great nephew.

---

1 Father Richard. **2** On right with brother Justice & mother Louise.
3 Sister Edith. **4** On left with Leslie Berlein. **5** His painting.

1

2 ‹‹‹
3

4

5

Gordon Paramore.   *Capt 8th Royal Berks*   *25th September 1915. Loos*

CAPT G. PARAMORE   PARAMORE · C·G

PARAMORE, C.G   CHARLES · GORDON · PARAMORE

C.G PARAMORE   C. GORDON PARAMORE

PARAMORE. C.G.

C.Gordon Paramore.   PARAMORE. C.G.

PEACOCK T. G. T. G. PEACOCK

T. G. PEACOCK

GORDON PEACOCK

T. Gordon Peacock

GORDON PEACOCK

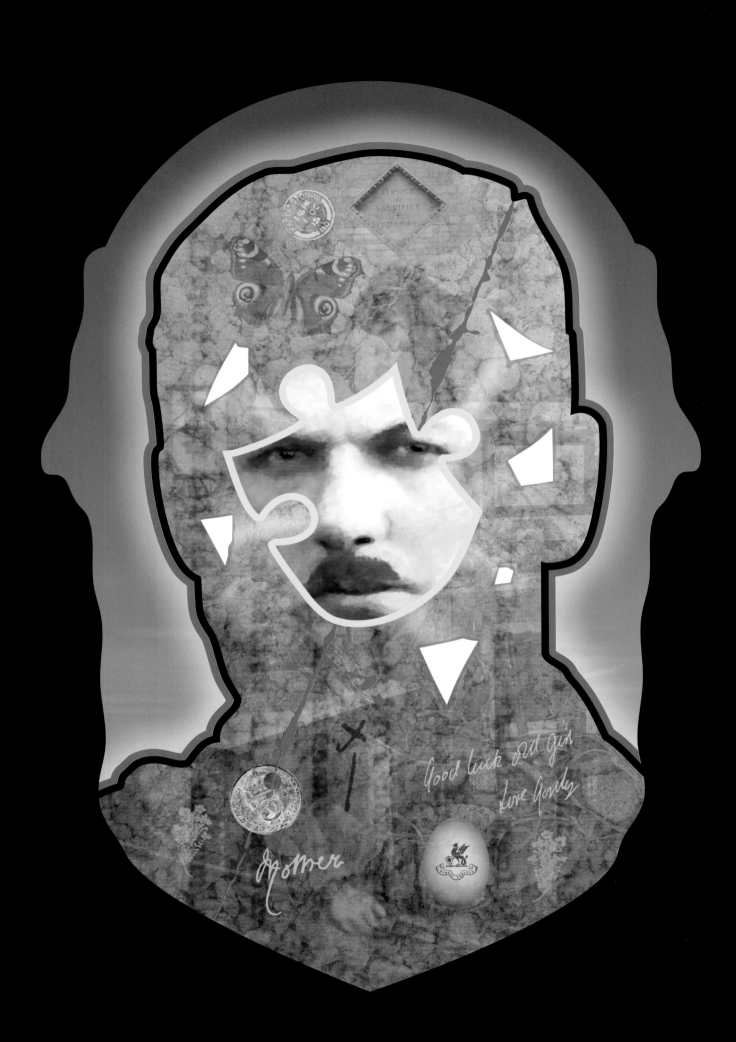

children
grandchildren
great-grandchildren
great-great-grandchildren
great-great-great-grandchildren

Lieutenant & Adjutant **Thomas Gordon 'Gordon' PEACOCK**

b. Sunday 8th October 1893 in Croydon, Surrey, England
d. Saturday 25th September 1915, near Hulluch, Pas-de-Calais, France (killed in action on the first day of the Battle of Loos)
Time on Earth: 21 years, 11 months, 18 days
Buried on battlefield, not found after war, no known grave, 5 known memorials

1830   1840   1850   1860   1870   1880   1890   1900   1910   1920   1930   1940   1950   1960   1970   1980   1990   2000   2010

He must have shown serious organisational abilities to be picked by my great-grandfather as his adjutant at the age of only 21. On the eve of the battle he remained up all night, comforting, encouraging and preparing his men. His body was identified by his mother's card in his hand along with 2 sprigs of heather and a threepenny bit with a hole in it. His younger brother Jack took his place in the family firm, Nurdin & Peacock, importing eggs and butter, and developed it into a massively successful cash & carry business. Jack only took two days off a year: Christmas Day, and Armistice Day – and on Armistice Day he was to be left alone to remember his brother. Even to his death 64 years later any mention of his brother reduced Jack to overwhelming sadness. Recently, the discovery of some long-forgotten trunks increased the number of pictures I had of Gordon from 9 to 61. My visit to copy these photographs led to such interest that I ended up giving a talk to 31 members of the family.

Stained glass window: Early on in my project I was working on artwork and chose the peacock butterfly rather than the bird to represent him. Subsequently, on the 82nd anniversary of the eve of his death, on a cold and misty morning, I was in the main cemetery at Loos and there was a peacock butterfly on the ground. In the winter of 2008, I was writing a presentation about Gordon Peacock when I found a peacock butterfly in my house. A year later, I found another peacock butterfly dead on my stairs – it was 8th October, and 8th October was not only Gordon Peacock's birthday but also the day on which his body was found on the battlefield in 1915.

—

1 Father Thomas. 2 Mother Maude. 3 Following the Victorian fashion of long hair for infant boys. 4 At back, with sister Coline, brother Jack, & half-brother Ronald.

1

2 ‹‹‹

3

4

Dear old Col,

Just a line to wish you good-bye. We're going into a big scrap and who knows? Anyway if you get this you'll know I am no more.

I wish I'd been a better brother to you but its too late to wish now isn't it? Sorry old lady I'd have liked to give you a good time, but I always thought there was plenty of time, and now it's too late.

I hope you'll have a good time. But be careful whom you marry. I should like to have seen you safely married to a good chap but there again regrets are useless. For heaven's sake choose a man when you do marry. Not a long-haired freak who's musical or artistic or something. They are always small-minded and spiteful. A good sportsman whatever his faults may be is broad minded and easy to get on with.

Well old girl – Best of luck. Good-bye. Lots of love from your loving brother Gordon

—

1 With sister Coline on right. **3** His last letter. **4** Coline's bible bookmarked with Gordon's photograph and with passages highlighted in I Corinthians Ch16. Underlined is "Death is swallowed up in victory". **5** With younger brother Jack & elder half-brother Ronald.

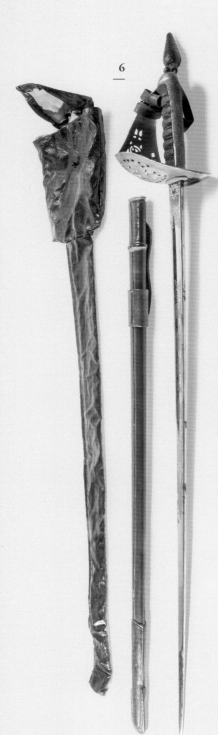

Gordon's Room

Gordon Peacock.

6 His sword, as worn in the photograph opposite, along with waterproof cover. **7** His empty bedroom (from a pre-war house catalogue). **8** This case sat on Jack's dressing table for the rest of his life. **9** Jack as Chairman of Nurdin & Peacock in the 1960s. **10** Jack's descendants and their spouses at Esher Village Hall in 2014.

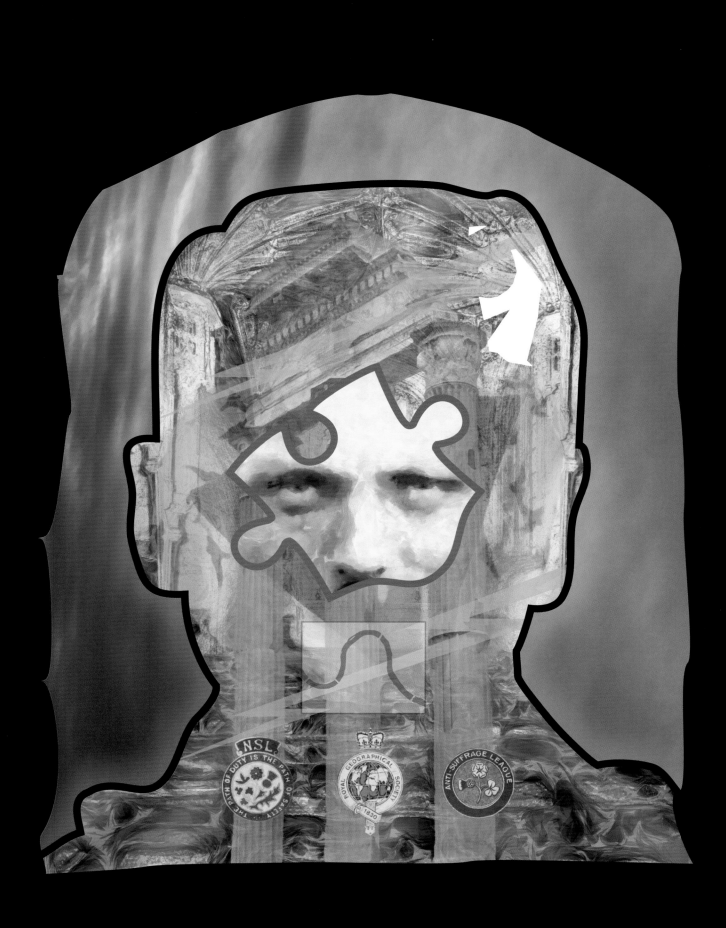

children ⸻
grandchildren ⸻
great-grandchildren ⸻
great-great-grandchildren ⸻
great-great-great-grandchildren ⸻

2nd Lieutenant **Richard Stephen Pierrepont 'Stephen' POYNTZ** later Captain

b. Sunday 25th November 1883 in Kilndown, Goudhurst, Kent
d. Sunday 9th March 1958 in Berkeley, Gloucestershire, England (old age)
Time on Earth: 74 years, 3 months, 13 days
Buried, no gravestone, no known memorial

1830 1840 1850 1860 1870 1880 1890 1900 1910 1920 1930 1940 1950 1960 1970 1980 1990 2000 2010

Pre-war he read Theology at Oxford (he was fanatical about the Boat Race and sulked for weeks if Oxford lost) and was a political speaker on behalf of the National Service League and the Anti-Suffrage League. Involved in half a dozen major actions during the War, he emerged without a scratch (and this annoyed him as he saw all his men dying around him). Became an instructor in 1917. After the War, he started a package tour business, first to the battlefields and then in Europe and around the World, teaching himself languages as required. Married late in life, his first child arrived when he was 54, and he became a school teacher at 60. For a Victorian gentleman he had a surprisingly modern outlook and thought Rock 'n' Roll was tremendous & highly amusing. He was buried near his family's ancestral home at Iron Acton (the first morning after I posted online about my project I found an email from Austin, Texas, telling me about his Poyntz ancestry going back to the 11th Century).

Stained glass window: He was a Fellow of the Royal Geographical Society, and had strongly held political beliefs.

—

1 Father Nathaniel. 2 In France during WW1. 3 Tour brochure.
4 On right, with mother Helen & siblings Helen, Alban & John.
5 Wife Eileen & son.

A TRIP DOWN UNDER
WITH
CAPTAIN R. S. P. POYNTZ
(Late Royal Berks Regt.)

and I request that I may be appointed to a temporary
f the war.

Usual Signature of Candidate.

IN LOVING MEMORY
OF
MERVYN PHIPPEN PUGH
BORN SEPTEMBER 15TH 1893
DIED APRIL 24TH 1961

THE PROSECUTOR

*The Life of M.P. Pugh
Prosecuting Solicitor and
Agent for the Director
of Public Prosecutions*

ALLEN ANDREWS

Foreword by Sir Norman Skelhorn, K.B.E., Q.C.
Director of Public Prosecutions

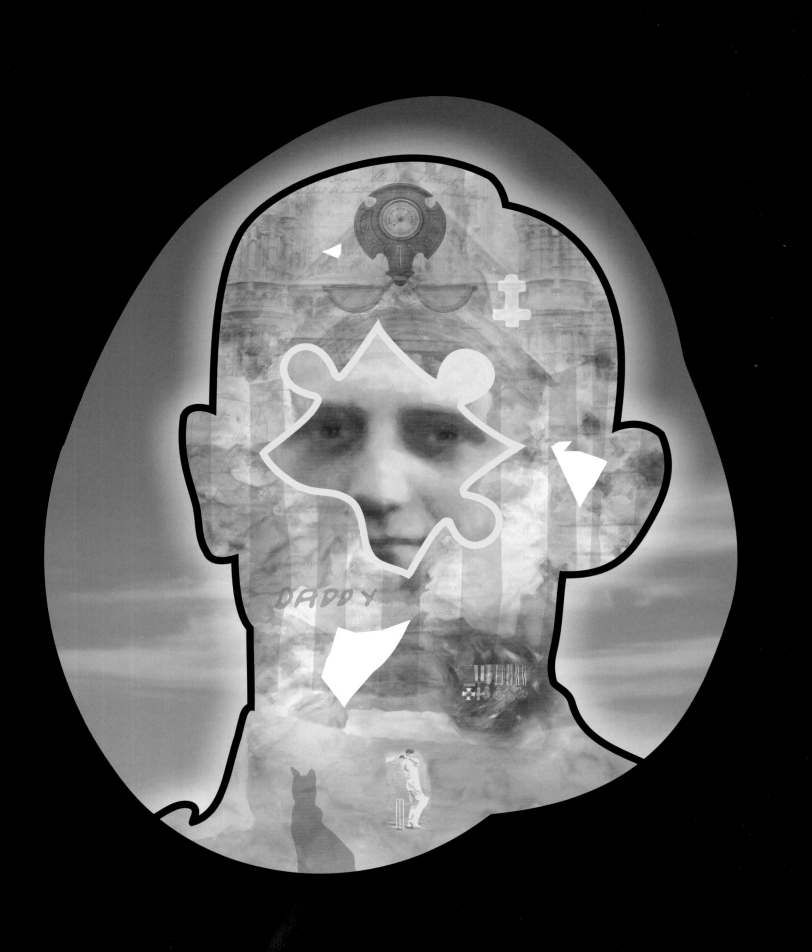

children
grandchildren
great-grandchildren
great-great-grandchildren
great-great-great-grandchildren

2nd Lieutenant **Mervyn Phippen PUGH** later Captain (acting Major), DSO, MC

b. Friday 15th September 1893 in Reading, Berkshire, England
d. Monday 24th April 1961 in Droitwich, Worcestershire, England (heart failure)
Time on Earth: 67 years, 7 months, 10 days
Cremated, ashes buried, gravestone, also a biography published

1830 1840 1850 1860 1870 1880 1890 1900 1910 1920 1930 1940 1950 1960 1970 1980 1990 2000 2010

Left behind when the battalion went to France, he was sent to join the 1st Royal Berkshires. The only one of these men still out fighting on the Western Front at the end of the War, and the most decorated for bravery. Buried by a shell in June 1916 that left him with face wounds and shrapnel in his left leg, he rejoined in 1917 to take part in attacks on the Somme (awarded the Military Cross) and then the Battle of Cambrai, and then in 1918 at the age of 24 he had had to take over command of the 1st Royal Berkshires during the German Spring Offensive (awarded the Distinguished Service Order), and later recovered from the Spanish Flu in time to take part in the last 100 days of attacks that ended the War. He went on to become a renowned Agent for the Director of Public Prosecutions in the Midlands, overseeing 110,000 cases including 100 prosecutions for murder. A huge character, tough but fun-loving, and revered by a family that includes Pugh the cartoonist from *The Times* & *The Daily Mail* and another grandson who was very kind to me when I was very ill. One of their prized possessions is the steel helmet that bears the bullet hole from where it saved his life and thus enabled their existence.

Stained glass window: The barometer was a wedding present from his Masonic Lodge, the "scales of justice" underneath actually being his reading glasses.

—

1 Father Henry. 2 Standing on left, in 1910 at the Moravian School in Germany, where he finished his schooling. 3 Mother Elizabeth.

1

2

3

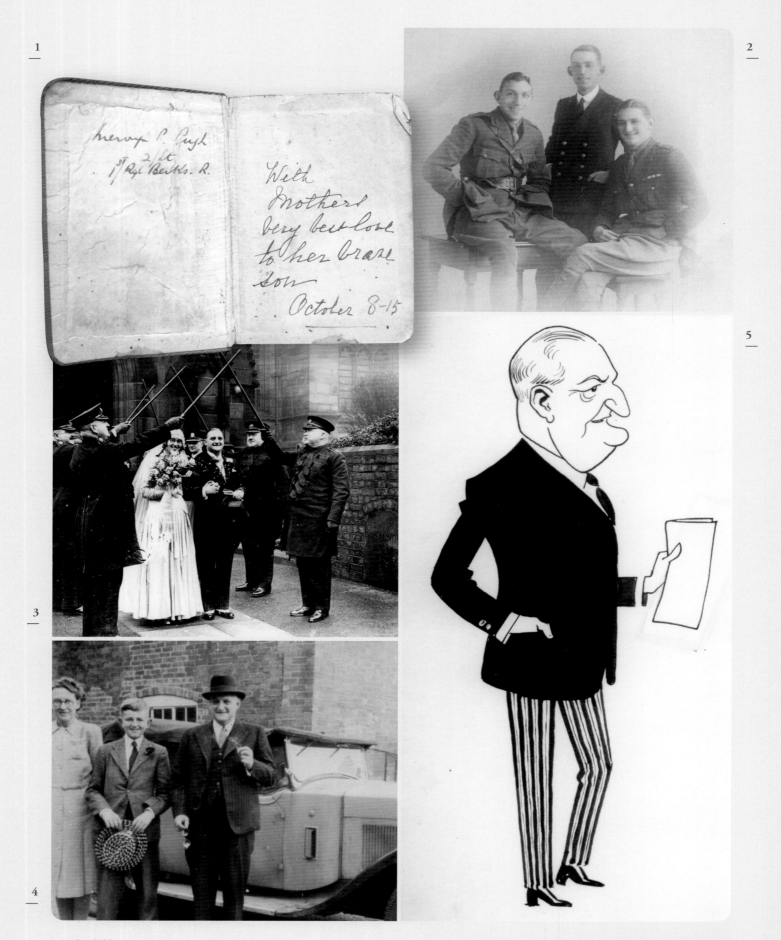

1 Pocket bible given to Mervyn by his mother on the day of his embarkation for France. 2 The survivors: on the right, with brothers Maurice (left) & Douglas after the War (two other brothers died in childhood). 3 His wedding to Vera in 1930, with police guard of honour. 4 With wife Vera & son John in the 1940s. 5 A view of Mervyn 'The Prosecutor', by unknown cartoonist.

Mervyn only wore his miniature medals when stipulated by the dress code for formal occasions. His full size medals have never been worn, and if he attended Remembrance parades it was only as an observer rather than a participant. He never talked about the War.

Son John.

Mervyn's 3 grandchildren & their spouses, and all 7 of his great-grandchildren, and above them the helmet to which they owe so much.

children
grandchildren
great-grandchildren
great-great-grandchildren
great-great-great-grandchildren

Lieutenant **Thomas Gerald 'Gerald' ROBINSON** later Captain, MC, French Croix de Guerre

b. Sunday 25th November 1883 in Brixton, London, England
d. Saturday 18th November 1972 in Burgess Hill, Sussex, England (throat cancer)
Time on Earth: 89 years, 2 months, 10 days
Cremated, ashes scattered, no known memorial

1830 1840 1850 1860 1870 1880 1890 1900 1910 1920 1930 1940 1950 1960 1970 1980 1990 2000 2010

He was left in reserve for both attacks at Loos. With some foresight he said to a fellow officer when facing out over No-Man's-Land in November 1915, *"The interesting point is that all of this is completely futile. Whatever happens, all of us, on either side, will be far worse off than before".* He managed to get through receiving some shell splinters in the face in March 1916, taking part in attacks on the Somme, and a bout of trench fever in September 1916. His fluency in French and German then got him a job on the Staff and ensured his survival. Returned to the silk trade (which he hated), had his wife of 14 years leave him (amicably) to become the secretary to the eccentric lesbian novelist Naomi Jacob, and then worked for inter-services intelligence during WW2 (including gathering information about the V1 launch sites – ironically his office building was hit by a V1 but he didn't notice as he was in the basement). His son was the last descendant of these men that I had to trace. After a very long and complicated search I discovered he'd changed his name and that as well as being a musical arranger for *Top of the Pops*, he'd orchestrated the scores for over 130 films. He told me how he'd taken his father to see *Oh! What a Lovely War*, and at the end when he'd turned, with tears in his eyes, to ask his father what he thought of the film, *"The Great War wasn't like that at all!"* was the affronted response.

Stained glass window: The gothic Z at top left is from the masthead of *Die Zeitung*. This was a German language newspaper (published in London during WW2) which he would read on the train despite the muttering of his fellow passengers.

—

1 Son Larry. **2 / 3** Wife Sadie in 1919 & in 1940s. **4** With son Larry at his 21st birthday party.

request that I may be appointed

war.

JSMRobinson.

Usual Signature of

2ND·LIEUT·T.G.ROBINSON

IN MOVING MEMORY
OF
AUBYN REDMOND ROUSE
SIXTH SON OF
HENRY JAMES ROUSE
BORN 8TH JANUARY 1882
DIED 12TH JUNE 1909

A.R.ROUSE

a R Rouse

children ———
grandchildren ———
great-grandchildren ———
great-great-grandchildren ———
great-great-great-grandchildren ———

2nd Lieutenant **Aubyn Redmond ROUSE** later Lieutenant

b. Friday 6th January 1882 in Marylebone, London, England
d. Monday 12th June 1939 in Bloomsbury, London, England (cancer of the caecum)
Time on Earth: 57 years, 5 months, 7 days
Buried, gravestone

1830	1840	1850	1860	1870	1880	1890	1900	1910	1920	1930	1940	1950	1960	1970	1980	1990	2000	2010	

His father was rewarded handsomely for building a bridge in Egypt, so handsomely that Aubyn and all 6 of his brothers went to Eton. It was a life of privilege, but also of Victorian restrictions – the children were to be silent at mealtimes with their parents speaking French to each other, and when the children had learnt French at school, the parents switched to Arabic. A rifle bullet broke his right forearm on the first day at Loos, leaving him unfit to fight and he transferred to become an Equipment Officer in the RFC and then the RAF. Returned to being an insurance underwriter at Lloyd's after the War. Met his wife ski-ing, though he was a curler rather than a skier. His wife re-married after his death and was shocked when she found she was pregnant for the first time at the age of 47. Her son by her second husband is the keeper of Aubyn's relics.

Stained glass window: His niece had fond childhood memories of listening out for the arrival of his car which he announced with a cuckoo horn, and on leaving he would always give her a half crown coin.

—

1 Father Henry. 2 As Eton Volunteer. 3 In Eton Field IX.
4 In the 1930s. 5 With wife Doris. 6 His memorabilia.

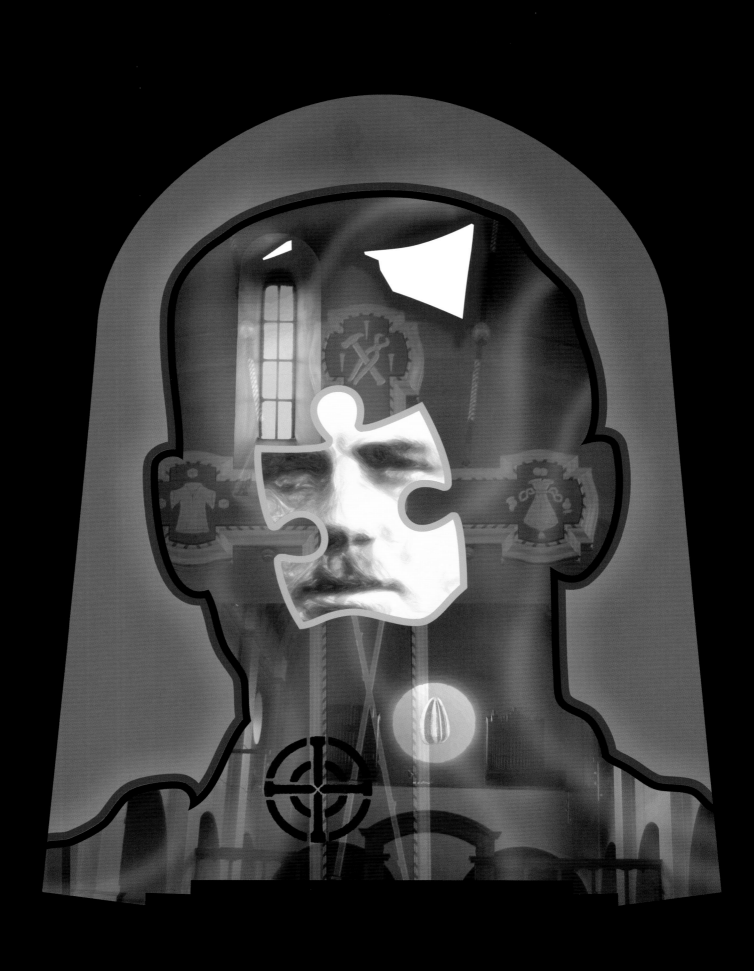

children
grandchildren
great-grandchildren
great-great-grandchildren
great-great-great-grandchildren

2nd Lieutenant **Clifford SALMAN**

b. Tuesday 1st August 1893 in Reading, Berkshire, England
d. Wednesday 13th October 1915, near Hulluch, Pas-de-Calais, France (killed in action in the 8th Royal Berkshires' second attack during the Battle of Loos)
Time on Earth: 22 years, 2 months, 13 days
Buried on battlefield, not found after war, no known grave, 8 known memorials

| 1830 | 1840 | 1850 | 1860 | 1870 | 1880 | 1890 | 1900 | 1910 | 1920 | 1930 | 1940 | 1950 | 1960 | 1970 | 1980 | 1990 | 2000 | 2010 |

Left behind when the battalion embarked for France, he arrived as a reinforcement 8 days before their second attack at Loos and was killed. It seems a far cry from the Theological College where he was following his vocation to become a priest at the time that war was declared. *"I don't want to go, but I feel I ought to"* are his words taken from one of two fulsome obituaries – from the College, and from the parish church in Reading where he was an altar server. He was a strong man with deep beliefs, but he wore them lightly and you can see that in the two informal pictures that remain of him. His only sibling Elsie lived to be 94 and never married.

Stained glass window: The background comes from photographs I took in the chapel where he worshipped at The College of the Resurrection in Mirfield.

1 Memorial to Clifford Salman in his parish church of St Bartholomew's in Reading (see his montage for close-up). It is above an encased Book of Remembrance that is dedicated to the memory of his father Arthur, for many years a church warden. Do those who pick up a processional cross or turn on a light switch in this corner ever stop and think of the man named on that stone tablet, of whom it was said: *"At the supreme hour he led his men and passed on before them. One who was behind him brought back the tidings that he died a very brave death; and who can doubt it? Clifford Salman has left an imperishable name."*

1

✠ REMEMBER O LORD THY SERVER
IN THIS CHVRCH CLIFFORD SALMAN
2ND LIEVT: ROYAL BERKSHIRE REGIMENT
WHO GAVE HIS LIFE FOR HIS COVNTRY
AT HVLLVCH OCT: 13TH 1915. AGED 22 YRS

IN
MEMORY OF
CLIFFORD SALMAN
2ND LIEUT R. BERKS REGT
OCT. 13. 1915
SERVER
R.I.P.

SALMAN C.   C. SALMAN
CLIFFORD SALMAN   C. Salman.
SALMON C
C. SALMAN   Clifford Salman
(Usual signature of

CYRIL·SPARTALI SPARTALI C.

CYRIL·SPARTALI CYRIL SPARTALI

C·SPARTALI · 2ND·LT · R·BERKS R · 1902

C·SPARTALI

U·C·SPARTALI

Cyril Spartali

C·SPARTALI

Cyril Spartali

(Usual signature of candidate)

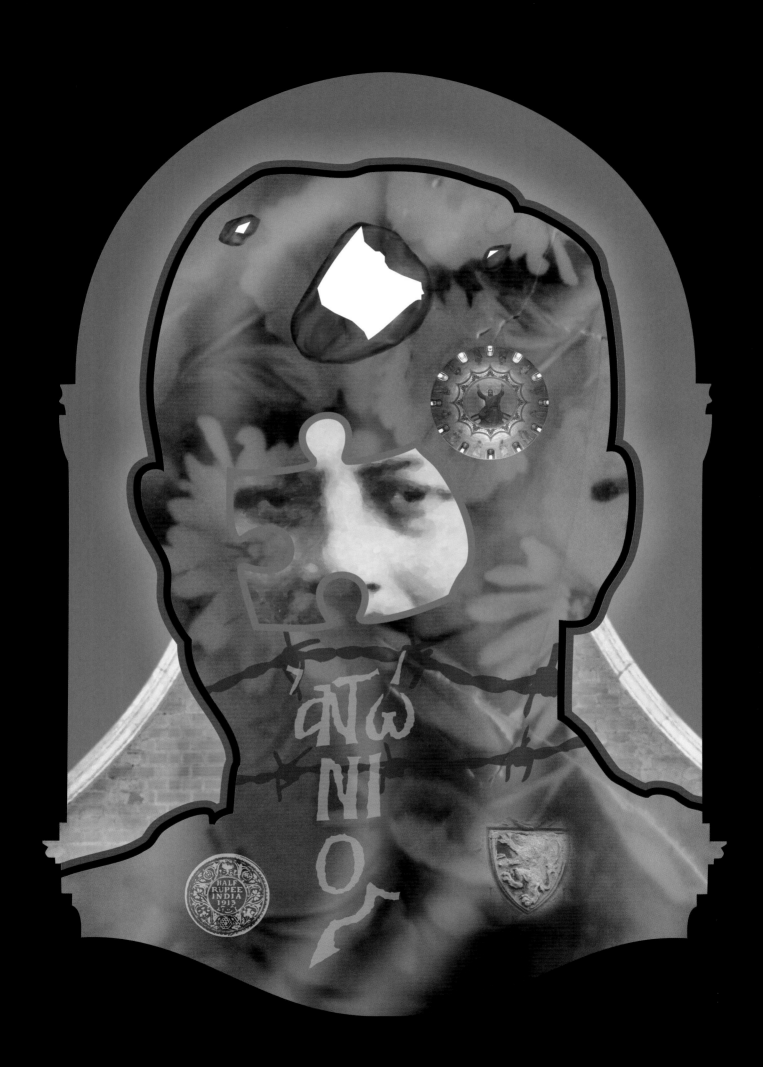

2nd Lieutenant **Cyril SPARTALI**

b. at 11.15 a.m. on Tuesday 10th July 1888 in Worthing, Sussex, England
d. Wednesday 13th October 1915, near Hulluch, Pas-de-Calais, France (killed in action in the 8th Royal Berkshires' second attack during the Battle of Loos)
Time on Earth: 27 years, 3 months, 4 days
Body never found, no known grave, 8 known memorials

Many of his ancestors came to England in the 1800s to escape the violence as Greece broke away from the Ottoman Empire, a precursor of the unrest in the Balkans that sparked WW1 (one great-grandfather was killed by the Turks on Chios). The family's wealth was no barrier to tragedy – his father died when Cyril was only 5, his twin sister when she was 22. He had just recovered from typhoid (contracted whilst working in his mother's family's great house of commerce in India) when war broke out. Held in reserve for the first attack at Loos, he was killed in the second. His family was practically wiped out in 4 months – his brother at Gallipolli, and his brother-in-law at Ypres 3 days after Cyril. Nearly all of his sister's descendants are planning to come to the exhibition.

Stained glass window: He is on memorials at Harrow School and in the Greek Cathedral in Bayswater (near his home, which is shown below the sky in the background).

—

1 / 2 Twins Irene & Cyril. **3** Father Demetrius. **4** Mother Virginia.
5 Sisters Effie & Irene. **6** Brother Bob. **7** Stepfather Edward.
8 Brother-in-law Ambrose.

children
grandchildren
great-grandchildren
great-great-grandchildren
great-great-great-grandchildren

Lieutenant **Donald Fenwick STILEMAN** later Captain

b. at 5.00 a.m. on Sunday 19th August 1894 in Ballater, Aberdeenshire, Scotland
d. Friday 3rd February 1989 in Salisbury, Wiltshire, England (heart attack)
Time on Earth: 94 years, 5 months, 16 days
Buried, gravestone

1830 1840 1850 1860 1870 1880 1890 1900 1910 1920 1930 1940 1950 1960 1970 1980 1990 2000 2010

Wounded in his first action at Loos (with shrapnel in his back and right foot), he was back with the battalion in January 1916 only to take a bullet in his right arm on the Somme in August 1916. This so damaged his ulnar nerve that it left him with what he termed a "dud hand" for the rest of his long life. Switched from studying history to forestry, starting out in the Indian Forestry Service and later working for the Forestry Commission in the UK. His life was dedicated to trees, and to his family who remember him with great joy and as a demon croquet player, even with his dud hand (he also managed to serve in the Home Guard during WW2). One of my favourite pictures is of him 10 feet up a ladder pruning trees at the age of 90 and with the use of only one hand. He was the longest lived of all the men in the group photograph and his epitaph says it all: *"Greatly Loved. Man of the Trees".*

Stained glass window: The sickle shaped tool was known as his "slasher" and accompanied him everywhere with his work. The crossword was filled out in his own hand and I couldn't believe my luck when I found the words *beautiful* and *guffaw* crossing each other – they just seemed so apt.

---

1 With parents & brother & sister. 2 In the front, 2nd from left, at University. 3 After wound on the Somme. 4 Mowing with dud hand. 5 With his children: Bob, Peter, Charles & Elizabeth. 6 Pruning, aged 90.

1

2 «««
3

4

5 «««
6

All Serene

Mostly I remember summer days,
the garden, the sailing sun, the mown lawn,
oddments for stumps and bails, a half-size bat,
a bright, real-leather cricket ball;
and pads and gloves for me.
After I'd asked for 'middle', marked the crease,
my Dad would bowl left-handed, underarm.
"All serene, boy?" he'd say, and then he'd bowl.
Maybe I was ten, he forty.
I got to know his wicked lobbing spin
and clouted him through apples trees to leg.
He'd shout for joy.
When his turn came to bat, one-handed,
against my speedy flailing overarm
he'd swing for six or out: and if he hit
we had to climb the fence and search the field.

He called his right hand 'dud'. He was blown up
on the Somme, invalided out,
and learnt to be left-handed. For us kids
the fascination was to feel the lump
of shrapnel lodging near his spine, and more
lumpish fragments sticking in his toes.
This German metal seemed no handicap
although, of course, the severed nerves and withered
right hand were.
He accepted these
disabilities as though inherited,
sometimes was annoyed because he couldn't grip

with the right hand, but persevered until
he'd mowed the turbulent grass, fixed the puncture,
staggered up the cliff precariously
with driftwood on his back and the dud arm
waving for balance.

So many magic pictures come to mind.

In old age, eyes blue as ever, he
loves reading, pottering in the garden,
sometimes wobbly on his pins
and waves that withered arm to keep upright:
He'll still climb trees for apples. He plays
croquet like an ace and often beats us all.
Me and my brothers he calls "Boy".
"Hello, Boy!" when one of us arrives.
Grandsons also qualify.
"What are you up to, Boy?" he asks Richard,
Christopher, Mark – the whole tribe: great-grandson too:
and "Girl" applies to daughter and granddaughters.
Strange the warmth this greeting generates.
Somehow it makes us all belong.

"And now your score is ninety three. Take guard!
All serene, Boy?"

Written by Donald's son Peter for the occasion of Donald's 93rd birthday. Peter got him to read in front of the whole family and it made him laugh like anything.

An inspiration: "The man who planted trees"

I thought I'd share with you a story that has provided an inspiration to me from quite early on in my project. During September 1997, I went on a trip with my flatmate, Jonathan, to visit the First World War battlefields for the second time. During our journey south from Calais, we stopped off in a wood to relax in the quiet sunshine. It really was the most fantastic place to be – an escape from the busyness and grey of Bristol in autumn. I talked about how much I enjoyed being amongst trees, how they had inspired some of my painting, and how I felt I ought to be doing something connected to trees – and Jonathan asked me if I had read the book *The Man Who Planted Trees*. I hadn't, but on our return I borrowed it from Bristol Central Library. It is a short book, originally written in French by Jean Giono, and illustrated with black-and-white wood-cut prints. The narrator tells the story of going walking in an inhospitable mountainous area of France in the early years of the Twentieth Century. He runs out of water and is lucky to find a shepherd who helps him out. He stays a while and observes the shepherd in his work and sees that every day the shepherd is planting acorns and seeds with the aim of growing trees in the barren landscape. Every day he does this. The narrator goes away, serves in and survives the Great War and returns to visit the shepherd, who is still planting trees. Many years later, the narrator visits the area again to find people enjoying a huge forest, that, unbeknownst to them, had been created by the quiet perseverance of one man – a man who knew his goal, and whatever the weather and whatever else was going on in the world just did what he had to do.

An inspiring story in itself, but not long after reading that I received a phone call that put the story in a new light. It was from the son of one of the men in the group photograph. A friend of the family had picked up the leaflet I'd left on the chairs at a conference at the Public Record Office. The leaflet gave an outline of my project and listed the names of all the men in the group photograph. The name "Donald Fenwick Stileman" had stood out and it wasn't long after that that I met his son and heard his story.

Donald Stileman was the son of the first Anglican bishop in Persia. His parents were often away for long periods and a lot of his childhood was spent with his grandparents and at boarding school. When the war started he was up at Cambridge reading history. The pictures of him sitting on the steps with friends show him looking quite laid back, and reports from fellow old boys of his school talk of him sleeping and drinking too much and occasionally turning out for the Dodos, one of the student hockey teams. I get the impression he didn't have any particular aim in life and was content to drift where the flow took him. Then the war came. He joined the Army, trained for the best part of a year, went over to France and was probably the first of the men in the group photograph to be wounded, right at the beginning at the Battle of Loos - and then, as already described, he was wounded again on the Somme and left without full use of his right hand for the rest of his life. After the war he seems to have gained a sense of purpose. Rather than go back to his history degree, he switched courses to study forestry. This also entailed a change of University from Cambridge to Oxford, which, given the rivalry between those two institutions, shows that it was a big deal and he meant it. After graduation he secured a job in the Indian Forestry Service, and from then on his two chief priorities were his family and trees. He got married out in India but on the arrival of his first son he moved back to England and joined the Forestry Commission. He wanted to provide the stable home environment that he himself had not had when growing up, and he dedicated his life to his four children (and in turn their families) and to his work with the Forestry Commission, determinedly overcoming his handicap. Even after retirement and within one year of his death at the age of 94, he was still working with trees. When I visited the family farm, his son took me into the garden and swung his arm round in every direction to show the trees that had been planted by his father – and not just a few isolated clumps, but great masses of woods – all planted by one man in spite of having a dud hand from wounds received on the Somme. Every member of his family that I talked to practically glowed with the remembrance of him and then of course there was his epitaph: "Greatly Loved. Man Of The Trees". If there was nothing else I took from this project, the story of Donald Stileman and *The Man Who Planted Trees* would have been enough to make the whole thing worthwhile. I have spent a long time in my own purposeless drifting, not knowing what my life was for. From a young age I have been very interested in the Parable of the Sower, with the idea of lives starting in different circumstances and leading their different ways. My project has given me a way of exploring what that means for people living their lives today. I may not have had my own children, or planted much in the way of real trees, but in the end it seems that my mission is to grow family trees and I've just got on with it. The path has not always been the easiest but I am beginning to see the rewards not just in terms of what it means to the families involved but also what it can mean to everyone.

DONALD FENWICK STILEMAN

1894 — 1989

GREATLY LOVED

MAN OF THE TREES.

F. M. Sumpster.

F. M. SUMPSTER

SUMPSTER F. M.

SUMPSTER Lt F. M. ROYAL BERKS.

Lieut **Frank Mariner Sumpster**

8th. Battalion Royal Berkshire Regiment.

died France, 21·3·1918

1899 ⚬⚬⚬ 1904

children
grandchildren
great-grandchildren
great-great-grandchildren
great-great-great-grandchildren

2nd Lieutenant **Frank Mariner SUMPSTER** later Lieutenant

b. Wednesday 15th August 1888 in Farnham, Surrey, England
d. Thursday 21st March 1918 in the area of La Guinguette Farm, near Alaincourt, Aisne, France
(killed in action on the first day of the German Spring Offensive)
Time on Earth: 29 years, 7 months, 7 days — Body never found, no known grave, 5 known memorials

1830   1840   1850   1860   1870   1880   1890   1900   1910   1920   1930   1940   1950   1960   1970   1980   1990   2000   2010

Having coming back from farming with his brother in Canada, he joined up, got married (his bride prettily attired in a costume of lotus blue silk moire), and shipped out to France in time to help reorganise the 8th Royal Berkshires after their disastrous second attack at Loos. Other than some time out for a gunshot wound to the shoulder received on the Somme, he served all the way through to the time he went missing. It took a year for him to be declared dead, during which time his wife received all sorts of contradictory reports. His only daughter was born a month before he died and by the time I found her she was in a home with dementia and I could only communicate with her via a solicitor. She said that at one time her mother had a lot of photographs of Frank but she was often too upset to talk about him and over the 44 years of her widowhood, the photographs were gradually destroyed. His brother's descendants knew little if anything about him.

Stained glass window: The outer frame shape comes from the war memorial of the Royal Grammar School, Guildford, on which he is named.

—

1 Guildford civic war memorial. 2 Holy Trinity Church, Guildford, Roll of Glory. 3 Royal Grammar School, Guildford, war memorial.

children ─────────
grandchildren ─────────
great-grandchildren ─────────
great-great-grandchildren ─────────
great-great-great-grandchildren ─────────

2nd Lieutenant **Edward Sidney Beaumont 'Teddy' TAVENER** later Captain

b. Sunday 29th July 1894 in Plympton, Devon, England
d. Monday 15th March 1976 in Guildford, Surrey, England (stroke & pneumonia)
Time on Earth: 81 years, 2 months, 16 days
Buried, gravestone

1830 1840 1850 1860 1870 1880 1890 1900 1910 1920 1930 1940 1950 1960 1970 1980 1990 2000 2010

The sole only child in the group photograph. Survived the war thanks to getting food poisoning in the trenches from eating a deteriorated tinned Maconochie's meat ration which left him unfit for active service (though he continued in an administrative role for the RAF to the end of the War). Enjoyed the colonial life as a conservator of forests in India, but found it a come down when he returned to the UK after Partition in 1947, and the scrap books he kept throughout his life were barely added to in the last 20 years of his life. A grand-daughter served in the Gulf War as an Army nurse, and a great grandson has served in Afghanistan as an Army doctor.

Stained glass window: The cross and globe symbol is from the parish magazine of the church where he was confirmed at the age of 63¾.

—

1 Parents Helen & William. **2 / 3** Father's parents William & Mary. **4 / 5** Mother's parents William & Ann. **6 / 7** Father's mother's parents. **8** Mother's mother's father's father. **9** As a boy. **10** In the RAF. **11 / 12** India.

1

2 / 3 ‹‹‹

4 / 5

6 / 7 ‹‹‹

8

9

›› 10

11 / 12 ‹‹‹

E. S. B. Tavener

IN LOVING MEMORY
OF
CAPT. EDWARD BEAUMONT
TAVENER "TEDDY"
1895 – 1975

M.B. THOMPSON

M.B. THOMPSON

MORICE BELL THOMPSON

M.B. THOMPSON Lieutenant
Machine Gun Corps.

MORICE. THOMPSON.

MORICE THOMPSON

M.B. THOMPSON

MORICE BELL
THOMPSON
LIEUT 8TH MACHINE
GUN CORPS
KILLED IN ACTION
MONCHY LE PREUX
MAY 3RD 1917

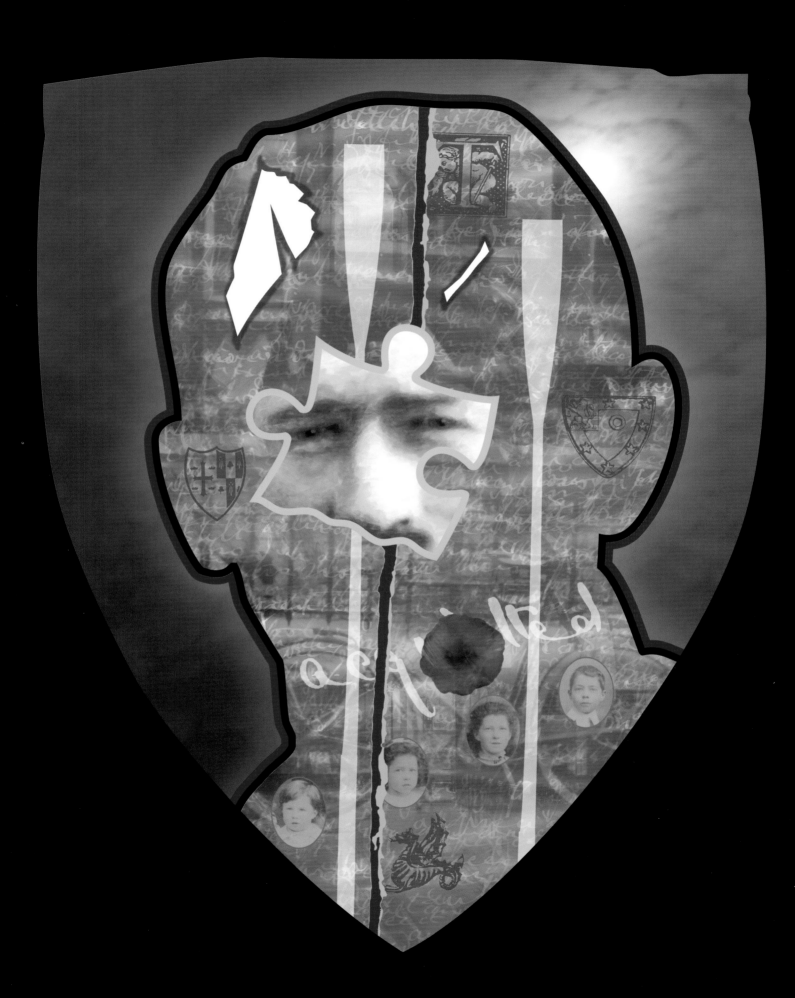

children —
grandchildren —
great-grandchildren —
great-great-grandchildren —
great-great-great-grandchildren —

2nd Lieutenant **Morice Bell THOMPSON** later Lieutenant

b. Thursday 31st December 1891 in Lucknow, India
d. Thursday 3rd May 1917 in the area of Monchy-le-Preux, near Arras, Pas-de-Calais, France
(killed in action with 8th Battalion Machine Gun Corps in an attack during the Battle of Arras)
Time on Earth: 25 years, 4 months, 4 days — Body never found, no known grave, 9 known memorials, also on a rugby XV shield at his school

1830 1840 1850 1860 1870 1880 1890 1900 1910 1920 1930 1940 1950 1960 1970 1980 1990 2000 2010

At around the time that the group photograph was taken he was acquitted at court martial of drunkennness and disobedience. His father's 6-page letter to the War Office tells of a culture clash between a career regular officer (my great-grandfather) and a young officer more familiar with civilian ways, and pleads for a transfer to another regiment. He eventually joined the Machine Gun Corps in France in August 1916, and was killed whilst trying to save a man who had been severely wounded. His niece in Tasmania has been one of the most valued supporters of my project. When I contacted her, she had never seen a photo of her uncle Morice and I sent her 70 (mostly copied from a family album held by a cousin in Scotland).

Stained glass window: He was an all round sportsman both at his schools and St John's College, Oxford, particularly excelling at rowing. A photograph showing him as captain of his school's coxed four is particularly poignant – all five of the boys pictured died in the War.

—

1 Father William, an ex Army Chaplain. **2** Fishing in India with brother Treffry & sister Ursula. **3** Mother Lucy died in 1912. **4** In bow tie at back with brother Treffry, & in front: Barbara, Brian & Ursula.

1

2

4

3

1 In the centre of a less-organised boat. 2 The St Edward's School Coxed Four on the water. 3 2nd from right, in the Eight for St John's College, Oxford. 4 In the window of his digs in Oxford. 5 With his men in the Machine Gun Corps.

The Coxed Four of St Edward's School, Oxford in 1910
This photograph was presented to the school by Morice, their
Captain. All are named on the School War Memorial.

Left to right:

Captain & Stroke: Morice Bell THOMPSON
    Lieutenant, Machine Gun Corps
    Killed in action at Monchy-le-Preux, France,
    on 3rd May 1917, aged 25
No. 2: Aubrey Noel CAREW HUNT
    Captain, Oxford & Bucks Light Infantry
    Killed in action near Arras, France,
    on 5th June 1916, aged 24
Bow: Cedric Donovan UPSTONE
    Second Lieutenant, Devonshire Regiment
    Died in hospital in Bombay, India,
    on 11th July 1916, aged 23
No. 3: Howard St John JEFFERSON
    Lance Corporal, City of London Yeomanry
    Killed in action at Gallipoli, Turkey
    on 5th September 1915, aged 21

In the front:

Cox: Basil William RAMSBOTTOM
    Lieutenant, Norfolk Yeomanry
    Killed in action near Hazebrouck, France
    on 19th August 1918, aged 22

W.H.CHALMERS	P.J.C.SIMPSON
C.E.R.BRIDSON	E.W.WARE
J.C.BUSH	J.A.T.CRAIG
J.B.BLAXLAND	L.J.E.C.FAIRWEATHER
F.R.HUDSON	B.W.RAMSBOTTOM
J.L.M.MORTON	G.C.TOWNROE
W.R.A.WAREING	F.K.HOLTON
D.C.B.BRIEN	B.L.JAMES
W.J.HARE	C.S.RANSON
R.H.RIDSDALE	M.L.G.RICHARDSON
E.W.ROSE	W.M.C.HUNT
J.L.CHALMERS	H.G.WILLIAMSON
E.G.F.PRYNNE	L.CASS
F.R.C.HAMMOND	A.V.CLARE
G.H.BICKLEY	E.HOBBS
A.N.C.HUNT	C.B.FORD
M.B.THOMPSON	P.C.OWEN
A.P.GREEN	R.T.HETT
B.W.PENNY	L.DAVIES
M.THORNELY	G.B.HUDSON
F.H.M.ROBERTSON	G.E.WILKINSON
H.St.J.JEFFERSON	E.A.CAVE·PENNEY
L.J.D.STANDEN	J.W.LEY
J.P.R.BRIDSON	G.L.STRANGE
W.H.DORE	B.R.H.CARTER
W.H.M.NORTH·COX	J.B.PARTINGTON
C.D.UPSTONE	H.EYRES
L.T.SEYMOUR	L.A.O'MEARA
M.E.KING	H.E.HUDSON
J.C.HYDE	J.H.SKENE

children ————
grandchildren ————
great-grandchildren ————
great-great-grandchildren ————
great-great-great-grandchildren ————

2nd Lieutenant **Henry Cyril 'Cyril' THORNE** later Lieutenant

b. Friday 26th August 1892 in Reading, Berkshire, England
d. Tuesday 27th June 1916 in the area of Carency, Pas-de-Calais, France
(killed in action with 1st Royal Berkshires whilst leading a night raid on the German trenches)
Time on Earth: 23 years, 10 months, 2 days — Buried, CWGC gravestone, 1 known memorial

One of the few true Berkshiremen in the group photograph, he went from single invoice clerk at the biscuit factory to married commissioned Army officer in 129 days. Conflicting reports of how he went missing meant that his 24 year old wife only heard he was dead two months later when communication was received from the Germans via the American Embassy: *'Lt. Cyril Thorne, Died. Effects are in our possession'*. Other than his grave, the only known memorial listing his name ended up in a store in Reading Museum some time after the closure of Huntley & Palmers' factory in 1976.

My contact with his family stirred an interest in him that had lain dormant through the silence of earlier generations.

Stained glass window: He was renowned in his local area as an all-round sportsman, his favourites being hockey and tennis.

—

1 Huntley & Palmers memorial. 2 Great nephew Graham.

Report 1: *Lieut. Thorne was in A Coy and we were attacking through Trones Wood to take the wood and the village. We did so and afterwards dug ourselves in outside the village. The Lt, however, was killed when in the centre of the wood by the 1st German trench, from MG fire. We always held that ground and I feel sure the Lt's body was buried by our own men, and I believe that the 16th Middlesex formed the burying party.*

Report 2: *Informant states that on June 26th or 27th at Vimy Ridge, Lieut Thorne led a bombing attack. After the attack search was made for Lieut Thorne all over the ground and the search was renewed the* next morning, *but nothing whatever could be found of him. Informant was one of those who went to search. The Medical Officer also made a thorough search over the ground. Informant's own opinion is that Lieut Thorne was taken prisoner, and he tells me that the Medical Officer was of the same opinion. Informant speaks of Lieut Thorne as a "very nice fellow".*

Report 3: *I was with him in a bombing raid at Vimy Ridge. I saw him with a Corporal and five men go in the German trench. None of them came back. The rest of us eventually retired. We sent out a search party afterwards but nothing was seen of them.*

1

2

LIEUT. C. THORNE.

Cyril Thorne

Usual Signature of C.

MAJOR D. TOSETTI, M.C.

DOUGLAS TOSETTI

D·TOSETTI D. TOSETTI MAJOR D. TOSETTI M.C.
ROYAL BERKSHIRE REGIMENT

DOUGLAS TOSETTI, M.C. MAJOR R. BERKS.

D TOSETTI

D. TOSSETTI

MAJOR
TOSETTI D. M.C.

Captain **Douglas TOSETTI** later Major, MC

b. Friday 6th July 1877 in Bromley, Kent, England
d. Thursday 21st March 1918 in the area of La Guinguette Farm, near Alaincourt, Aisne, France (killed in action on the first day of the German Spring Offensive)
Time on Earth: 40 years, 8 months, 16 days
Body never found, no known grave, 7 known memorials, also named on a team photograph in his school's cricket pavilion

1830 1840 1850 1860 1870 1880 1890 1900 1910 1920 1930 1940 1950 1960 1970 1980 1990 2000 2010

He had an Italian name but his father was a German who had come to England in 1867. Douglas joined the family business in the champagne trade and played a lot of sport, including turning out for Essex against a touring lacrosse team from Toronto in 1902. He fought all the way from Loos (where he was wounded in the leg on the first day and won the Military Cross) to the Somme to Passchendaele to the German Spring Offensive. By that time he was Battalion second-in-command and he sacrificed himself to locate a German machine gun that was pinning his men down. Letters received by his father show how universally loved he was and how he was worshipped by his men (and not only because when acting as President of Courts Martial he was inclined to show them sympathy and tend towards lenient sentences, despite repeated tellings off from his Divisional Commander).

Stained glass window: He was a great pal of Charles Bartlett, who, writing from the mud of the trenches, referred to him as *"Dug"* and this is how he signed a note added to one of Charles Bartlett's letters.

---

1 Mother Julia. **2** On left with father Max, brother Gilbert & sister Lilian. **3** The hazards of the wine trade for father Max.

1

2

3

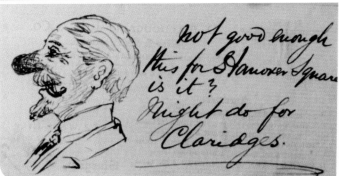

not good enough this for Hanover Square is it? Might do for Claridges.

Younger brother Gilbert was also a gifted sportsman, in fact from the records he was more gifted than Douglas, particularly at cricket. He scored a century for Essex against Lancashire in 1902 and was in the Essex team that beat the touring Australians in 1905.

1 A refreshing change from the posed shots of the era, with possibly sister Margaret. 2 As a gunner in the Honourable Artillery Company (1900-1904, part-time). 3 On right, playing lacrosse for Woodford, Essex. 4 At the seaside, in Sheringham, Norfolk, 1909. 5 On left, with Charles Bartlett.

At the time of the opening of the German Spring Offensive on 21st March 1918, Douglas was the last of the men in the Group Photograph still to be serving with the 8th Royal Berkshires. These letters to his father were copied and sent to Cecil Cloake who by this time was back in England.

They are from men who knew him well:

- his commanding officer, Lt Col Robert Dewing, DSO (who was killed the day after writing this letter)
- Rev Arthur Longden who had been the 8th Royal Berkshires' chaplain from September 1915 to February 1918
- Private Fred Bailey, MM & Bar, who was Douglas' runner (and survived the War)

3.4.18

Dear Mr Tosetti,

I am afraid I have a very sad letter to write you.

Your son Douglas, was killed on March 21st. He was with us in the front line, when the Bosch attack started and did most gallant work in a reserve Trench which we were occupying. When we were eventually forced to evacuate the Trench he moved with others along a communication Trench. The enemy were close behind us and we had to stop and fire to hold him up every few yards.

Your son was hit as he was firing at the enemy over the parapet of the Trench. He must have died immediately as he was quite dead when I came along very soon afterwards.

He was literally worshipped by all the men in the Battalion especially as he had been with them so long and knew so many of them personally.

His loss will be felt very much by everyone, and I myself feel I have lost not only a very valuable officer but one of the best friends a man could want. His first thoughts have always been for the men and he was never happier than when he was with them.

The Battalion has lost many good Officers and men, but we feel here that the Bosch is now held up and that the tide will turn.

I must end by offering you the very deepest sympathy from myself and from all ranks of the Battalion in the great loss you have suffered.

Yours sincerely
R. E. DEWING. Lt. Col.
Commanding 8th Royal Berkshire Regiment.

11th April, 1918.

Dear Sir,

I have just received your letter of the 5th, enquiring about the death of Major Tosetti. It was on the morning of the 21st March when our Battalion was attacked and we were holding a trench successfully for about three hours when we found we were cut off and surrounded, and it was necessary to fight our way back to a reserve trench, so Major Tosetti took command of some men to fight their way through, while the C.O. took command of the men that were holding them back from the front of us. All was going well until they got a Machine Gun trained on us; then the Major sacrificed his life to locate the gun to put the gunners out of action. He was shot through the head and chest, and was killed instantly and I can assure you, if it had not been for his bravery in locating the gun, hardly any of us would have got away. I am sorry I am not allowed to inform you of the place where it occurred, but I hope that, at some future time, I may be allowed to let you know. I hope you will accept mine and the remainder of the Battalion's deepest sympathy in your great loss. It was a great loss to the Battalion, when he was killed, as he undoubtedly was one of the finest and bravest officers serving his Country. I am very sorry to inform you that our C.O. was killed instantly, after being wounded about ¼ hour beforehand on 4th April after we had beaten off another attack. If there is anything I can inform you about and you would like to know, I will be pleased to do so.

Believe me, dear Sir,
Yours faithfully,
Pte. F. BAILEY, 19013

7.4.18

Dear Mr Tosetti

I was very much distressed on seeing my paper yesterday to read of Douglas' death. I was with the Battalion from September 1915 until quite recently when they went away from us and I have heard no details of how they got on in the great battle. We ourselves have not yet got into it. To you I know Douglas' death will come as a very great blow, for knowing him as I had the privilege to do I am certain that you must be tremendously proud of him. He was loved by everyone who knew him both officers and men, not only in the Battalion but in a much wider sphere and his departure is a very real loss to us all. Many of us hoped that he would have had command of the old Battalion, and I am sure that it was only because of his reticence and gentleness that he was not chosen for this honour.

Kind hearted to the last degree he always seemed to find good in everyone, and so was unable to punish anyone who erred unless it really was a crime and then it seemed to hurt him intensely to have to inflict any punishment. He was without exception one of the most tender hearted and generous men I have ever met and with it all one of the most fearless. He was always full of thought for the comfort and welfare of his men – seeing to them and their needs before he thought of himself even after the most strenuous days work.

How he fell I do not know, but I am certain it was during the course of duty. His example will always remain with us to remind us of what a true gentleman should be. May God grant him rest and peace, and to us re-union with him and his life hereafter. May He also give to you and your family that comfort which human words fail to give.

I am,
Yours very sincerely,
ARTHUR LONGDEN
(Chaplain to the Forces).

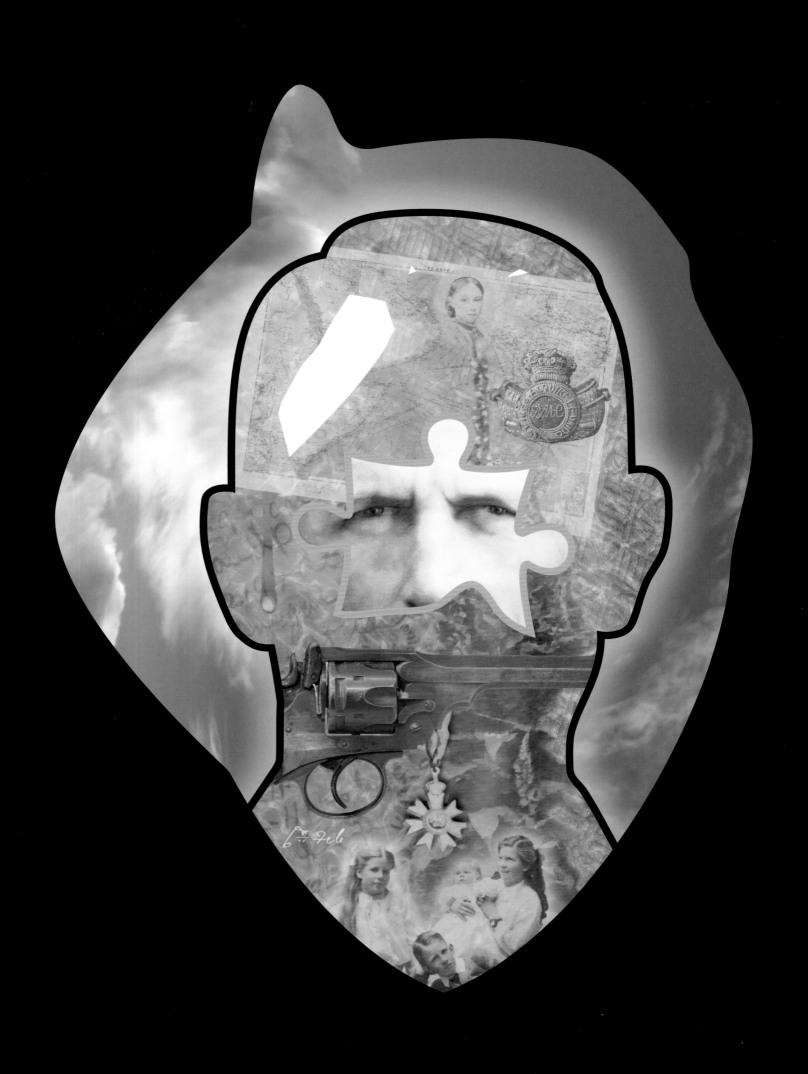

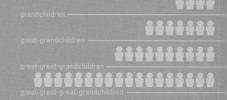

children —
grandchildren —
great-grandchildren —
great-great-grandchildren —
great-great-great-grandchildren —

Colonel **William Crawford 'Bill' WALTON** later Brigadier General, CB, CMG

b. Tuesday 15th November 1864 in Karachi, India (now in Pakistan)
d. Sunday 9th May 1937 in Weybridge, Surrey, England (blood clot in lung, heart failure)
Time on Earth: 72 years, 5 months, 25 days
Cremated, ashes scattered, no known memorial

1830 1840 1850 1860 1870 1880 1890 1900 1910 1920 1930 1940 1950 1960 1970 1980 1990 2000 2010

Losing his mother when he was 3 and his father when he was 17, he had to make his own way in the world and went straight from school to RMC Sandhurst. After service in the Burma War (where he lost the sight of his left eye in a riding accident), he spent the next 29 years in the Indian Army rising to be Commandant of 104th Wellesley's Rifles. Back home in the UK in 1914, he was on the unemployed list and on the way to retirement when war broke out. Raised and trained the 8th Royal Berkshires and led them in action at Loos, where he had to rally his men in the smoke and the gas and shot 2 Germans at close range with his revolver. Reclaimed by the India Office, he was removed from the battle after 3 days and posted to command a Mobile Column in Aden against the Turks. Retired as a Brigadier General and served as a district councillor with particular interest in education and young people's welfare. An absolutely dedicated, if somewhat strait-laced, public servant, he was not one for the limelight and he had a quiet funeral with

no military honours. It was his daughter (my grandmother) who showed me his letters from the trenches and eventually led to the revival of his memory within the family.

Stained glass window: 6th February 1884 was the date of his commission (so consequently his seniority date), and he was promoted Captain on 6th February 1895 and Major on 6th February 1902. Coincidentally his daughter (my grandmother, at bottom left) was born on 6th February, as was one of his great-granddaughters.

—

1 Father Hubert. **2** Standing in centre behind his stepmother Harriet, with siblings in back row: Robin, Tony, Daisy & Hubert, and in front row: Lena & May (mother of Charlie Watson from the Group Photograph). **3** Mother Diana.

1

3

2

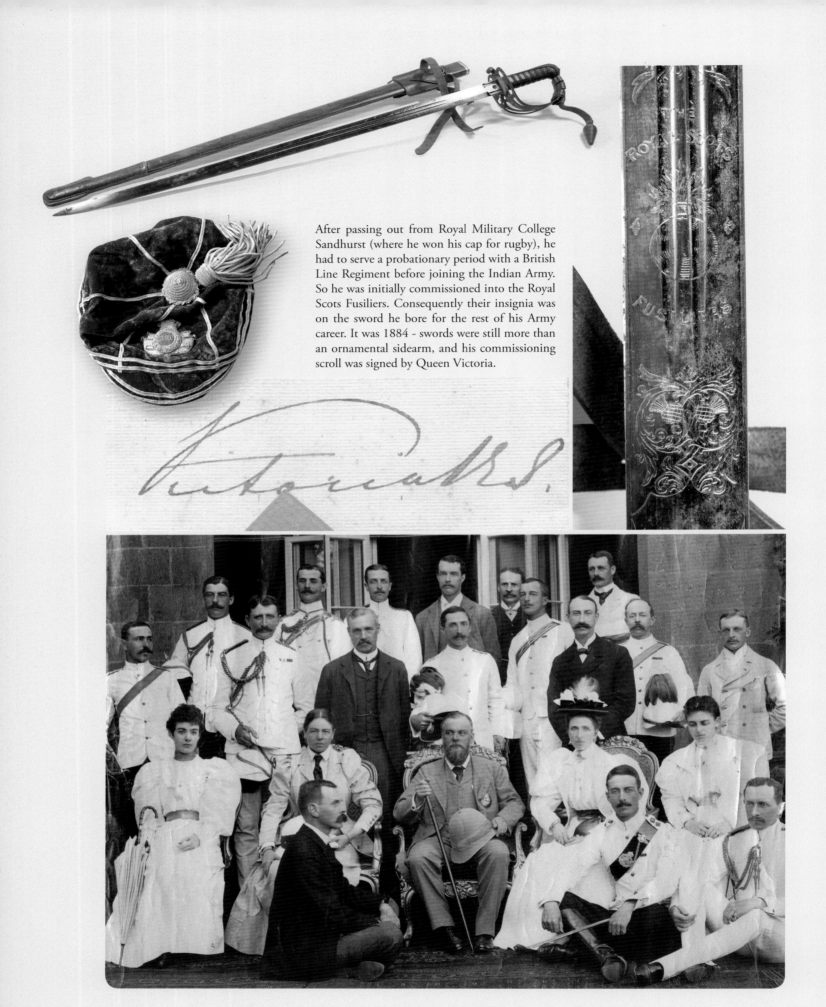

After passing out from Royal Military College Sandhurst (where he won his cap for rugby), he had to serve a probationary period with a British Line Regiment before joining the Indian Army. So he was initially commissioned into the Royal Scots Fusiliers. Consequently their insignia was on the sword he bore for the rest of his Army career. It was 1884 - swords were still more than an ornamental sidearm, and his commissioning scroll was signed by Queen Victoria.

At front right with dark cross belt, in 1899, as commander of the Guard for the Viceroy of India, Lord Elgin, who is seated in the centre. What is that man doing at bottom left?!

In December 1910 William Walton was involved in the arrangements for the visit of Crown Prince Wilhelm of Germany to Bombay, as described in these extracts from a letter that his wife wrote to their eldest daughter:

On Wednesday Daddy & I left here at quarter to 6 and drove to Bandra and went by train to Bombay to dine at Government House and meet the German Crown Prince. It was most interesting and I had a very good place with only Prince Henry the XXXIst of Reuss between me and the Crown Prince so I saw him very well. He was brought round before dinner and introduced to each of us in turn and shook hands – the slowest handshake I ever got! Daddy had to meet him that morning on the steps of the Pier when he landed and he had told me how slowly he shook hands with him then and how steadily he looked right into your eyes. ... The tables were arranged like this:

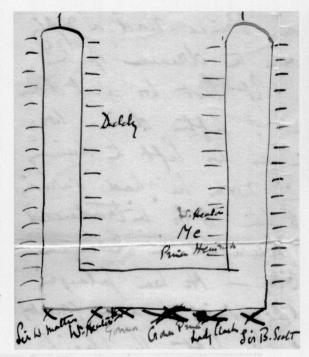

Crown Prince Wilhelm - was known as Little Willie in Britain. He went on to command the German 6th Army during the War. His great-grandmother was Queen Victoria and his descendants are still in the line of succession for the British throne.

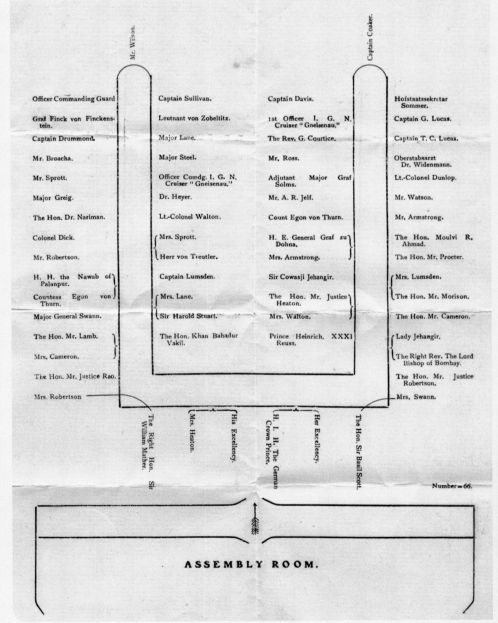

Nobody sat opposite the Crown Prince. Prince Heinrich was a German, he is the Consul General in India and was delightful. He told me such a lot about the Crown Prince and about Germany and he spoke English perfectly. When we finished the soup up jumped the Crown Prince and proposed the King Emperor's health and the Band played God Save The King and we drank it standing up of course. We had no sooner sat down than the Governor rose and proposed the health of the Emperor of Germany and again the Band played and we drank to his health. Again in a minute the Governor rose and made a long speech to the Crown Prince and proposed his health and the Crown Prince had a reply saying it had always been the dream of his life to visit India. At last we sat down and the Fish came in! After dinner we had to curtsey to him as we left the dining room and in the drawing room he had various people brought up to him to be introduced again and he looks so interested in every one and such a cheery boy. He was playing Polo yesterday and Daddy said had a great reception there. Today he left. ... I thoroughly enjoyed my evening and found it all most interesting. There were about a dozen of his Staff with him and 66 people altogether at dinner. Much love and many good wishes to you all for 1911 from your loving Mummie.

1 With wife Emmy, Diana & Patricia, 1901. 2 With Emmy, Diana, Patricia & Billy in Bexhill-on-Sea, 1910. 3 Outside Buckingham Palace for awarding of his CB, with Billy, Emmy, Patricia & Diana, 1922. 4 Giving away his daughter Diana, 1928. 5 Armistice Day parade with grandson John, 1933. 5 Holding my father Ben, 1934.

William Crawford Walton and all his descendants, left to right, from top to bottom:

Diana/Dan,

Patricia/Peg,

William/Billy,

Alexander/Sandy,

John,

Richard/Dickon,

Belinda/Bin,

Timothy/Tim,

Mary/Poo,

Benjamin/Ben/Bun,

Edmund/Ned,

Philip/Phil,

James/Jamie,

William/Willie,

Charles/Charlie,

Andrew,

Anna,

Jennifer/Jenny,

Jonathan/Jonny,

Nicholas/Nick,

Richenda/Chen,

Orlando/Lando,

Frederick/Freddie,

Francis/Frankie,

Darius,

Storm,

Atticus,

Roya,

Cyrus,

Elizabeth/Lizzie,

Dougal,

Freddie,

Finbar,

May,

Oliver,

Arlo,

Sarah,

Edward/Eddie,

Kestrel/Kes.

prior to, or during service.

ture ...... Charles R Watson

mpleted by Medical Board.)

children
grandchildren
great-grandchildren
great-great-grandchildren
great-great-great-grandchildren

2nd Lieutenant **Charles Randolph 'Charlie' WATSON** later Lieutenant

b. Sunday 15th October 1893 in South Hornsey, Middlesex, England
d. Tuesday 22nd March 1977 in Vancouver, British Columbia, Canada (heart failure & prostate cancer)
Time on Earth: 83 years, 5 months, 8 days
Cremated, ashes scattered, no known memorial

1830 1840 1850 1860 1870 1880 1890 1900 1910 1920 1930 1940 1950 1960 1970 1980 1990 2000 2010

Four years into this project I discovered that he was my great grandfather's nephew – one of my grandmother's 31 first cousins – and when I met his son in Montreal I worked out that he was the taker of the fantastic photographs that were in an album stored with my great-grandfather's letters and which show the men of the battalion during training. He developed a disease of the foot that kept him out of the Battle of Loos, but was there to witness the aftermath and never got over it. Going back to Canada to ferry Chinese coolies over for the war effort, he then lost himself in the British Columbian interior for a while before settling and becoming chief accountant at a shipyard. He had an excellent baritone singing voice and a tremendous memory for songs and jokes and foreign languages which could make him delightful at parties, but behind it was a deep-seated depression and his interest in photographing people seems to have been abandoned.

Stained glass window: His solace was gardening – to such an extent that people would stop outside his house in admiration. He planted 3 or 4 layers of bulbs so that they'd be flowering throughout the summer.

—

1 Father George. 2 Mother May née Walton. 3 Nearest the camera, pre-war with Seaforth Highlanders of Canada. 4 On left, in the British Columbian interior. 5 Wife Ruby. 5 Son Bill.

1
››› 2

4

5 ‹‹‹

6

children
grandchildren
great-grandchildren
great-great-grandchildren
great-great-great-grandchildren

2nd Lieutenant Cyril Arthur WILLIAMSON later Lieutenant in WW2

b. Saturday 23rd June 1888 in New Romney, Kent, England
d. Sunday 16th May 1954 in Oxford, Oxfordshire, England (heart disease & pneumonia)
Time on Earth: 65 years, 10 months, 24 days
Cremated, ashes scattered, no known memorial

1830 1840 1850 1860 1870 1880 1890 1900 1910 1920 1930 1940 1950 1960 1970 1980 1990 2000 2010

Hand and foot injuries sustained whilst in saw mills and on the railways in Canada before the war meant that he barely passed the Army medical and this ultimately saved him because on the three occasions he went up to serve in the trenches he had to return unfit. After the war he became a rep for Dunlop in Latin America but the Depression brought an end to his idyllic lifestyle with redundancy and a return to England followed by the suicide of his wife. He appears a shadow of his former self in the photographs after that. Served in supply (and possibly intelligence?) in WW2 and remarried to a translator 21 years his junior. One son had a charmed life in the Navy in WW2, surviving 2 Arctic convoys, the relief of Malta, and 7 opposed landings as a landing craft commander. His other son won 5 Oscars for technical achievement as a movie camera engineer, inventing modern slow motion photography and IMAX.

Stained glass window: The 3 clubs are on the Williamson coat of arms but also represent to me his brothers Hubert, who died as a young boy, and Harold, who was killed on the 1st day of the Somme, and a grandson who died of injuries sustained at birth.

—

1 Back, with brother Hubert & sister Annie. **2** Right, with brother Harold. **3** With wife Louise. **4** As Dunlop overseas rep, with son Peter. **5** Centre, son Peter on landing craft. **6** Son: camera engineer Geoff.

1
››› 2

3

4

5 ‹‹‹

6

H. V. Woodford (1912), Lieutenant, Berkshire Regt., killed
in action in France, January, 1916.

Harold. V. Woodford
Usual Signature of

children
grandchildren
great-grandchildren
great-great-grandchildren
great-great-great-grandchildren

2nd Lieutenant **Harold Vivian WOODFORD**

b. Monday 23rd January 1893 at Epsom, Surrey, England
d. Wednesday 13th October 1915, near Hulluch, Pas-de-Calais, France (killed in action in the 8th Royal Berkshires' second attack during the Battle of Loos)
Time on Earth: 22 years, 8 months, 21 days
Buried on battlefield, not found after war, no known grave, 8 known memorials

1830	1840	1850	1860	1870	1880	1890	1900	1910	1920	1930	1940	1950	1960	1970	1980	1990	2000	2010

The son of an explorer (who wrote a book entitled *A Naturalist Amongst the Head-Hunters*), he spent his formative years in Australia and the Solomon Islands (where his father became Resident Commissioner) before going to public school in England. Left a Malayan rubber plantation to join up. Went missing in action only 8 days after rejoining the battalion in France. 10 weeks later his body was found just 20 yards in front of the British wire by a lance corporal who had gone out into No-Man's Land one night to search for British dead. Amongst the items recovered from his body was a prismatic compass engraved with his name that I was shown by his niece in Australia 88 years later.

Stained glass window: The crown motif is from the war memorial of Hawkesbury Agricultural College in Australia, where he went to study in 1912 (and where he saved a fellow student from drowning).

---

1 Father Charles in 1880s. **2** Father Charles in 1890s. **3** On mother's lap, with brother Charlie. **4** With mother Florence on the veranda.

1

2 «««

3

4

1 Will Bissley (right) sitting next to Donald Stileman (centre) with Billy Haynes (left) & Harold Cohen (front) during a battalion sports day in 1915. Donald Stileman survived the other three in this group by 72 years.

CONNECTIONS

1
—

I'm often asked whether there have been any connections in recent times between the families of the men in the Group Photograph. There don't appear to have been many (at least not until I started contacting everyone), but one early discovery was that one of Gordon Peacock's great nieces had been taught by my cousin's first husband. No, not a close connection and they never knew about it. More recently I moved to Norfolk and in asking around for some bedding I ended up being given the sheets and pillow cases of one of Hugh Cassels' nephews - they were in the possession of a friend who had been involved in clearing his house after he died. Also in the move to Norfolk, I inherited a Koi pond. I knew nothing about Koi and rang a company in the Yellow Pages for advice. Nick came out to look things over and we saw each other on and off as I needed pumps or advice or huge amounts of fish muck removed. He even put up a poster advertising my Open Studio that included an image of the Group Photograph. But it wasn't until 2 years after our first meeting that I heard from a cousin of his who was coming over for a family wedding in Norfolk and worked out that Nick was the great great nephew of Douglas Tosetti.

The most significant connection I have found, though, is that Donald Stileman's granddaughter Lizzy and Will Bissley's great-grandson Nick met whilst at Plymouth University in the 1990s. Both joined Exeter University Officer Training Corps and they ended up sharing a flat. One weekend Nick went with Lizzy to stay at her parents' house. In honour of her involvement with the Army, she had been given her family's copy of the Group Photograph and had just had it framed. She was showing Nick how amazing it was to see her grandfather as a Second Lieutenant when even more amazingly he pointed out his own great-grandfather - his family had the same Group Photograph. Both went on to be commissioned and left the Army as Majors last year.

MEMORIALS

||||||||||||||||||||||||||||||||||||||||||||||||||||||||||||||||||||||||||||||||||||||||

Remembrance has been a central theme to this project. Some of these men have been forgotten. Their names appear on memorials - "Their name liveth for evermore" - but that is all there is. Sometimes it's because their family has died out, often it's because there have been splits in families and the present day is overwhelming the past. Even those who are remembered are often only remembered as outlines because the pain of their loss meant that they were not talked about. It is in their memorials that you can see what their loss meant at the time of their death.

A number of these men have individual memorials dedicated to them or are named on their parents' graves, but they also belonged to communities that remembered their loss by including their names on the memorials for schools & colleges & universities & villages & towns & cities & churches & synagogues & workplaces & other institutions. The name of one of these men appears on 12 memorials.

On the following pages you will see some of the most beautiful and poignant memorials that I found during my research. The three big stained glass windows hold particular value as there is no-one left from their families to remember them directly. As in life, so in death luck plays its part. It helps to have rich relatives who can afford beautiful memorials but even that is no guarantee, as time has all sorts of ways of destroying the past. One of these stained glass windows ended up being judged on its monetary value and was split up and shipped to whoever would buy it, forgetting the heartache of a mother and a father who wanted to leave a beautiful reminder of their son in perpetuity.

Those who die young and in wars are often remembered, at least in name, whereas the survivors who made it through to old age can sometimes disappear from sight. In the case of the Group Photograph, over half the survivors have no known memorial. In fact I was told by a member of staff in a crematorium that in England today 70% of people are cremated of whom only 30% have memorials.

In the end, though, people are remembered for the extraordinary. For a lot of these men it is the extraordinary things that happened to them. For some it is the extraordinary things they did, and sometimes the extraordinary thing was as simple as showing people how much they loved them. The best form of remembrance is in how we live today – striving to learn from the mistakes of the past and following the good examples of those who have gone before us.

To the glory of God, and in loving memory of Harold Charles Linford Keable, 2nd Lieut. 8th Service Battalion Royal Berkshire Regiment, younger and dearly loved son of Charles Henry Keable, Vicar of this Parish and Constance Mary his wife, who gave his life at the battle of Loos, Sept. 25th 1915, aged 26. This Chapel is given by his Parents and Brother.

Harold Keable
St Peter's Church, Wrecclesham, Surrey.

Tod Hobbs
Richmond Presbyterian Church, Surrey
(church now an apartment block
& window has been sold:
centre panel is in Japan,
side panels are in Canada).

WISDOM   POWER   JOY   FAITH

NOT BY MIGHT   NOR BY POWER   BUT BY MY SPIRIT   SAITH the LORD   OF HOSTS

TO THE GLORY OF GOD   AND IN LOVING MEMORY OF   BASIL PERRIN HICKS Lieut   8th British R?W?H? GAVE HIS LIFE   AT LOOS SEPT 25 1915 AGED 22

Basil Hicks
St Peter's Church, Bushey Heath, Hertfordshire.

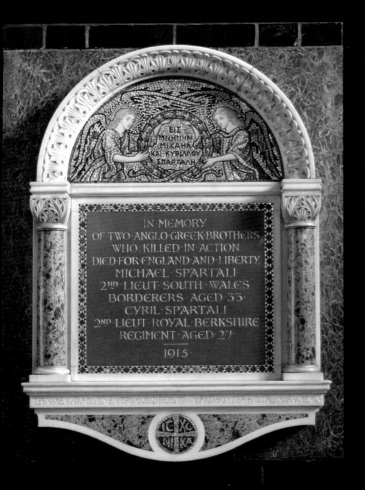

Cyril Spartali
St Sophia's Greek Orthodox Cathedral,
Bayswater, London.

Hugh Cassels
Clayesmore School,
Iwerne Minster, Dorset.

NOBLE. W.M.
PALK. J.W.M.
PALLING. W.L.
PARAMORE. C.C.
PARHAM. W.M.
PARRY. W.H.L.

CLOSING THOUGHTS

Before saying anything else I will make a plea for you to write down your family history - ask questions, dredge up the memories, and commit it to paper before it is too late. So much is lost and, for me, history is not a dead subject or something just to be done as a hobby as a way to find interesting stories to tell. It is an essential part of human existence - our personal & family history and the history of the society in which we live define how we interact with the World. Yet often our grasp on our history is rather shaky and is full of myths and half-truths that for a large part go unquestioned. This is no more clearly shown than in views of the First World War.

Looking at the men in the Group Photograph and what happened to them, what is there to learn? When they were growing up, and even right up until the beginning of the War, they can have had no conception of what was about to befall them. For all the sabre-rattling over many years, it would have seemed inconceivable that such an all-encompassing and all-devouring wave of destruction could sweep them up and lay waste to the civilised peoples of the Western world. Most of them had lives of material comfort and in the optimism of the Edwardian era it must have seemed as if that would continue forever. History shows, however, that human beings are not very good at predicting sudden and big changes, whether that is at a personal level or on a global scale - and if there is one thing I have learnt from this project, it is that "Anything is possible".

Often the phrase "Anything is possible" is used in a flippant way, particularly when talking about seemingly impossible things. But truly extraordinary things do happen that seem to fly in the face of anything leading up to them. For these men it was the First World War, and history is full of horrible destruction that might have been avoided if the people leading into it had really understood the vastness of the horror that was possible.

Of course it is not just bad things that are possible and human beings are equally unable to believe that life-changing good can hap-

pen too. A friend of mine grew up in East Germany. At the age of 13 she visited Berlin and standing on the Wall looking over towards the West, she thought, "I will never be able to go there". And the next year, the Soviet Union collapsed, the Wall came down, and she could. Donald Stileman from the Group Photograph went into action on the Somme in August 1916 and as he lay there with a terrible bullet wound in the arm and shells and machine-gun fire killing people all around him, he must have thought, "I am never getting out of this alive" - but somehow he did and went on to live for another 72 years - and unsurprisingly one of his sayings was "Never give up".

On a less extreme level, this project should have been impossible - and I've been told that many times, not least by family historians who were struggling away at one family tree, let alone 46. When I began, all of my research was with paper records in archives. It took hours of laborious searching to produce tiny nuggets of reward. And then the Internet came and suddenly I was able to connect with other researchers around the world who could help me, and I could put up a website that led people to get in touch, and then gradually more and more information came online along with searchable databases growing year on year. The ceaseless development of computer technology meant that by the time I got round to working up my artistic ideas, in particular my animated film, it had become possible to do them myself on a computer in my home. I also started out with very little money and there were times along the way where little became zero, and my efforts to attract funding led to nothing. At one point I was working long hours as a chef and getting nowhere on any level. Near to despair, I sat down and decided to write a list of things I wanted to do with my life. Top of the list was completing this project. So I just started getting on with it as best I could, and then out of nowhere I came into some money that enabled me to fully pursue it. And then eventually I met a man in the shape of Piet Chielens who could make things happen.

Along the way it has been hard not to be overwhelmed by the death and sadness that I encountered as I researched these men and their families but in amongst it all I was inspired by some extraordinary life stories that showed that individuals can make a difference even as the World is going mad around them. Each of us is born with talents and abilities to make a unique contribution to the World. It is sometimes hard to know what they are but if something burns brightly within you as something you must do, get on with it. It may not seem logical to anyone else, it may not even seem logical to you, but if it really speaks to you, just get on and do it. Do extraordinary things in the World before the World does extraordinary things to you, and don't let logic get in the way of a beautiful idea.

The World needs beautiful ideas whether they be scientific, artistic or political. Competing empires have been replaced by competing economies which are looking to expand infinitely in a finite World of limited resources. Nationalists make policies based on which particular geographical areas people are born in rather than on their qualities as individuals. People mistake the behaviour of the governments of countries for the behaviour of all the people of those countries. People slavishly follow dogmas without questioning their foundations. Comfortable people stick their heads in the sand at the sufferings of others. So much of the media seeks to stir up conflict and make a story out of it. Military action is seen as the solution to conflicts. Religions founded on deep spiritual ideas have been hijacked as a means to cause division. These are the sorts of behaviours that led to and sustained the First World War and they are the sorts of behaviours that cause wars now.

The men in this Group Photograph did what they thought was right with the beliefs that they had learned from their families, from their education, from the press and from the institutions and leadership of their country. They were prepared to sacrifice themselves for those beliefs and many died as a result.

Today we are lucky to have the freedom to ask questions and the resources to find answers that are closer to the truth. We can communicate with like-minded people in our own countries and around the World. Each of us can make a difference if we choose to do so. I hope that what you see in the exhibition and in this book makes you think about your own place in the World and in time, and encourages you to do what you can to make sure that what happened to these men never happens again.

Lizzie, great-great-granddaughter of William Walton.

THANKS

One thing you learn from doing a project like this is the importance of saying "Thank you". In 21 years of research and travel, I have been helped by enough people to fill this book. Being a completist and knowing the value of every contribution, I would love to list every single person. In the end, though, I've had 18 days to lay out the majority of the pictures and text in this book from materials I've collected/generated for the exhibition, and with limited space in the book I've been faced with the decision of whether to do voluminous thanks or include more pictures. The pictures won and the more detailed thanks will have to wait till the book of the "Making Of" this project. So, apologies to the many who are left out, but here goes. Not all of those named are still in this world, but they will always be with me.

My parents, **Ben & Sue Tatham** - their incredible generosity made this whole thing possible, as did sticking by me even when not understanding what the hell I was doing with my life.

Vanessa Watkins has remained convinced that this was all going to work out and has been a true friend, even if she won't stop quoting Goethe at me.

The National Archives has been the best of all the archives I've been to, always striving to provide a better service for researchers.

Colin Fox (who wrote my first reference when contacting the families) and his research group, especially **Mac McIntyre** & **John Chapman**, were extraordinarily generous in the sharing of their research into the Royal Berkshire Regiment. For those who want more military history than this book can give, I refer you to John's website: www.purley.eu

John Bourne greatly encouraged me and wrote my second reference after the death of Colin Fox.

Bill Cumberland sent me the picture at top left - it has been my touchstone ever since.

There have been so many family history researchers out there who have had a hand in this but the stand-out ones who have gone beyond the call of duty have been **Pam Hendy**, **Tony Valentine**, **Richard Renold**, **Margaret Clarke**, **Claudia Cole**, **Greg Ball**, **John Noel**, **Heinrich Nuhn**, & **Markus Detemple**.

Jonathan Hayter accompanied me on my second trip to the battlefields, incinerated his tent and told me about *The Man Who Planted Trees*.

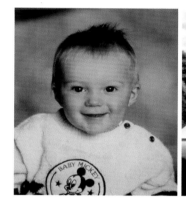

Tony & Max Ball accompanied me on my third trip to the battlefields, including the great exhaust pipe debacle. Max had just been born when I started this project, and this year has graduated, as in the above pictures.

Nikki & Ian Taylor gave me the first opportunity to show my animated film during Surrey Open Studios and made suggestions that vastly improved it.

David Yarham was the first person to book me for a presentation, starting the ball rolling again with my project after a lengthy hiatus and leading to all subsequent presentations.

Jim Witherspoon showed the DVD of my animated film in his gallery which led to **Sue Heath** booking me to show it at **Mundesley Junior School** who led me to seeing what my work could mean to young people.

Norfolk Library Service provided gainful employment and solace in the friendship of work chums and customers at **Fakenham Library**, as well as giving me extended leave this year, without which this exhibition would have been impossible. Special thanks are due to **Judith Bell** & **Ann Keeble** for having the foresight/madness to take me on in the first place and for being instrumental in booking me for my first presentations in Norfolk libraries.

Mac Graham through quality chattings helped me to focus on what was important and how to achieve this result.

The archivists and officials of so many schools and colleges and churches and other institutions with war memorials have opened their doors to my searches.

Long-term enthusiasts have been **Chris Budleigh**, **Patrick Miles**, **Cicely Bilverstone**, **Sally Wright & Paul Bunkham**, **Paul Mann**.

Diana Larman, having seen one of my presentations, invited me to **St Mary's School, Cambridge**, and so started a friendship with her and with the school that has transformed my outlook on this project.

My neighbour **Matt Skillings** knocked on my door regularly and took me out for walkies (& talkies) that were vital during the years of work in my hermitage.

Sally Webster brought the eyes & ideas of an artist to discussions about my work and her kindness was with me all the way during my illness.

Paul Ebdon also stuck with me when I was ill and is quite simply the best friend a man could have, even if he has put me off a lot of foreign travel by his film selections and will insist that I work in papier mâché. He & **Alan Schmidt** lent their artists' eyes to weekly viewings of my stained glass windows and boosted me with enthusiasm in bucketfuls.

Adrian Blake helped me to learn to trust my gut feelings and the conviction of his support even managed to convince me that I was on the right course.

The last year just would not have been possible without **Jan Campbell** wanting to see what I was working on, enthusing about what she saw and seemingly not minding having her ears bent as I talked on and on about my struggles.

Piet Chielens is an incredible man with a beautiful instinct and a clear eye. It was his enthusiastic response to my approach and his decision to hold this exhibition that formed the backbone of my work over the last four years and have seen it to fruition. His team at **In Flanders Fields Museum** have done a wonderful job of putting everything together, with particular thanks going to **Annick Vandenbilcke**, **Margot Brulard**, & **Lidia Giacomini** for their Herculean efforts in organising the Gathering of the families, and **Birger Stichelbaut** for taking the new group photograph.

Klaus Verscheure managed to coax a performance out of me for the introductory films in the exhibition along with cameraman **Didier Lenglaert** (& both introduced me to the pleasures of van-sitting in Hulluch), and then did an even better job in the editing suite with **Ernest Verscheure**.

Manu Veracx, the Black Box King, and his team at B.AD made my ideas and designs into a fantastic reality beyond my dreams. **Jan D'Hondt** took the beautiful pictures of loaned objects that are in this book.

I have purposely left till last any mention of the families of all of the men in the Group Photograph. None of them asked for me to parachute out of the blue and poke my nose into their lives, and the welcome and help I have received in so many cases is what has been the absolute foundation of this project. The first three I met were **John C Cloake**, **John Peacock** and **Charles Stileman** and all three absorbed my greenhorn stumblings about and helped me on my way in the beginning - without their welcome this may never have happened. For the years of support and the loan of irreplaceable family heirlooms, I am enormously grateful to: **Brian Berlein**, **John N Cloake** (who also helped so much with the text in this book), **Ann Constable**, **Nick Constable**, **Kathy Goode**, **Hugh Lee**, **Ed Pugh**, **Jonathan Pugh** (who also drew the beautifully apt cartoon on this page), **Peter C Lawrence**, **David Peacock**, **Keith & Joan Presswell**, & **Jill Sinclair**. Thank you to **Peter Stileman** for allowing me to include his poem to his father. In addition to their interest & support, particular (& much appreciated) generosity has been received from: **Penny Andersen**, **Fay Koza**, all of **Gordon Peacock's great nieces & great nephews**, **Louis Phillips**, **Nigel Pugh**, **Paul Smallwood**, **Mairead Da Silva**, **Frances Watson**, **Jim & Jane Williamson**. Chief enthusiasts & supporters & information givers have been: **David & Anne Allen, Derrick Anderson, Gina & John Anderson, Larry Ashmore, Barrie & Stephen Ayling, Kim & Ray Baker, Zoe Barclay, Betty Barnes, Julian & Tony Bartlett, Tamsin Beadman, Anthony & Alma & Tess & Claire Berlein, Helen Binckes, Doreen Boden, Lynne Brotchie, Mike Bull, Iain & Hugh Cameron, Di Campbell-White, Ruth Catherineau, Andrew Clark, Bob & Lorna & Mavis Clarke, Clare Clifford, Michelle Cooke, Joan Crampton, Ken Creed, Edward Curtis, Biddy Diamond, Vic & Peter & Mike & Brian & Andy Dobson, David Falconer, Joy & Bob Field, Susan & Martin Fisher, Pip Florance, Donald & Simon Fraser, Mary Galloway, Susan Gardner, Gill Grigor, Ned & Roberta Hamond, David Hayes, Peter & Andrew & Ted Hewitt, Rod Hinkel, Gay Hodge, James Horn, Peter Hull, Margaret Joseph, Diana Keable, Elizabeth & Tony Kendall, Louis Klemantaski, Peter G Lawrence, Jillian Lemmond, Christopher Long, Diana Loo, John Macdonald, Rosslyn Macphail, Nigel & Mimi & Popsy Marsh, Chen McCalla, Michael Millard, Vera Mitchell, Shirley Monnington, Jeremy Montanaro, Cathleen Morawetz, Tom Morgan, Jill Nash, Geoffrey Negus, Betty & Franciszka Ozog, Tony Paramore, Robbie Peacock, Steve & John Poyntz, Judith Poore, John Pugh, Edwina Rapley, Celia Randell, Gay Redman, Brenda Ribton, Linda Rix, Eleanor Rolston, Inez Ross, Tibby Seddon, Merylyn Shaw, Mary Smyth, Lizzy Stileman, Joyce Svensson, Kit Sykes, Peter & Graham & Jayne & Maurice & David Thorne, Alex Tosetti, Hazel Vaughan, Laurie & Mary Vincent, Bill Watson, Alan Whytock, Jack Wilcock, Peter Williamson, Bridgett Woodford-Smith**.

Many others not listed here are coming for the new Group Photograph. Thank you, every single one. May you live in interesting but peaceful times.